JESUS
Never Fails

The Story of Roger and Margaret Fox,

Missionaries to Japan

Margaret Fox Shaiebly

ISBN 978-1-0980-7720-4 (paperback)
ISBN 978-1-0980-7721-1 (digital)

Christian Faith Publishing, Inc.
832 Park Avenue
Meadville, PA 16335
www.christianfaithpublishing.com

Printed in the United States of America

CONTENTS

FOREWORD

Roger and Margaret Fox served as missionaries for forty-four years with the Far Eastern Gospel Crusade / SEND International. They spent eighteen years in Japan, beginning right after World War II, with the goal of bringing the gospel to the Japanese and planting a national church.

Their journal is chronicled in *Jesus Never Fails*, starting when they were young. They met in Baltimore in 1943 when they were teenagers, and they fell in love while he followed his dream of being a pilot in the army air corps and she pursued her dream of being a missionary in Borneo.

Their story continues with Roger's journey to the Far East during the war in a fighter plane and Margaret's desire to be a missionary and attending Bible school to obtain the educational background she knew she needed. Half a world apart, they wrote hundreds of letters back and forth, sharing every thought. He was willing to go with her on her missionary adventure to Borneo just because he wanted to be with her.

But God had other plans for their lives. In 1950, after getting married and finishing Bible college, they packed up two young children and a few meager belongings and headed out for Japan on a freighter out of San Francisco. Two weeks later, they arrived in the port of Yokohama ready for the new adventure on which they had embarked.

For the first five years, they lived isolated from any other English speakers and struggled to learn the Japanese language, ways, and customs while starting a national church. For the next five-year term, they learned other ways to reach the Japanese and built upon their experiences to determine the best ways to plant a national church with a national pastor.

After two terms on the field of learning different ways to reach the Japanese, they were determined to work themselves out of a job at the end of their third term by starting a national church and leaving it in the capable hands of a national pastor along with members of the church.

Jesus Never Fails, which was Margaret's guiding principle for her life, is their story. Follow along to understand how God molded them to be the people they became to do the things they did, through prayer, by having faith and trusting Him in all things.

Gary Fox

CHAPTER 1

A Happy Childhood

Fathers, do not provoke your children to anger, but bring them up in the discipline and instruction of the Lord.

—Ephesians 6:4 (NAS)

Roger grew up in a family of five children—Earl Seymore, Winnie Louise, Stanley Theodore, Irving Victor, and Roger Wesley—in Totowa Borough, New Jersey, which is about twenty-five miles northwest of New York City. The house was small by today's standards, but it was a happy and sometimes extremely crowded home, from what I had been told, with children and sometimes grandchildren moving in and out.

Mama Eva Fox was a fun lady, who liked to play practical jokes on guests who visited at her table. One of her favorites was to place a balloon under a guest's plate, then slowly inflate it using a small rubber hose. She would pump up the balloon a bit, raising the unsuspecting guest's plate, causing them to squeal. Mama would act so innocent when asked about it.

Papa George Fox was very quiet and very sweet with a nice sense of humor. When Mama Fox would prepare a meal that Papa didn't like, he would say, "That was good, but please don't make it again."

Spaghetti was popular at family gatherings and all who entered the family learned to enjoy it, too. Totowa was a predominantly

Italian area of New Jersey. For many years, some family would make the sauce that everyone loved to eat, and they would go about the neighborhood, selling it to those who wanted it. Everyone knew everyone in the community. The mailman knew everyone and shared births, marriages, and death announcements along his route.

Papa drove a horse and buggy when he started working for the Grand Union Tea and Coffee Company. Some of Roger's favorite days were going with Papa on his route and help deliver the tea and coffee. Neither Papa nor Mama were coffee drinkers, but Papa enjoyed the selling just the same. When automobiles became popular and affordable, Papa traded in his horse and buggy for a small truck that was especially nice on rainy and snowy days.

As the children grew, the bedrooms got smaller. The two older boys put up a tent in the backyard and had some cots and made that their sleeping headquarters for all seasons of the year for several years. The younger boys eagerly waited for the oldest brother to go to college so they could have a turn living in the tent. Because of the age difference between Earl, the other siblings, and Roger—eighteen years from oldest to youngest—he was too young to really enjoy the fellowship with them as he grew up.

His sister Winnie was his first grade teacher. He was instructed to call her by her married name, Mrs. Young. One day, he called her "Toots," his pet name for her, and the class burst out laughing. He was more careful after that.

Even so, Winnie thought that Roger could do no wrong, but the boys had other ideas. Mama said Roger enjoyed the basement with the few toys that he had and a few tools to work with. A hammer and screwdriver were always his favorite tools. He would make all sorts of boxes and shelves with any wood he could scrounge. Mama called him a "tinkerer," for he was always making something from wood and tinkering with all sorts of things.

Church played an important part in Roger's growing up. Mama was a preschool Sunday teacher for many years. She loved to read Bible stories for the children at the Totowa Borough Methodist Church. Creatively, she made all sorts of things out of nothing that were a means of taking the Bible message home. A walnut, for example, would be carefully cracked open, cleaned out and a verse tucked inside and sent home for Mother and Father to help their child memorize Jesus's Word for the next Sunday school class.

Papa was the sexton of the church beyond his tea and coffee job. A sexton takes care of a church buildings and property and often rings the church's bell during services. He volunteered his time, and it was a labor of love.

The family all went to Sunday school and church, morning and evening services, and also prayer meeting on Wednesday nights. When Roger was young, he remembered two women coming to the church and sharing God's Word. He recalled his mom and dad, several brothers, and his sister went to kneel at the front of church. It was a special week of meetings. Roger recalled going home and asked Jesus into his heart, but he didn't feel any different and thought it didn't take. That experience happened to him many times in his early life. He wanted something to happen and wondered what it would be.

Roger enjoyed school and was a fine student. By the time he was twelve, he was working in a hardware store. That wasn't his first job. He had worked as a delivery boy in a corner grocery store, and he enjoyed the treats he received with the pennies he was paid. The hardware store really intrigued his curiosity, and he had many learning times.

A gentleman who lived behind the small grocery store also loved wood and always was making something out of cherry wood. That was a learning time too. Roger loved deliveries to his home so that he could watch some of the making process. We have had in our home for many years a Japanese (blue) block print that is framed by cherry wood from this man's artwork.

Roger played football in high school. He wasn't the biggest boy, but he worked hard to be on the team. He had a young lady in those days named Shirley. He really liked her at the time, but God had other plans for him. One time, his dad included Roger's girlfriend's family in a family gathering in a fancy restaurant. When the meal was finished, Papa left a tip on the table. As the family was leaving, Shirley's mother, who hadn't seen Papa leave a tip, screamed across the dining area, "Dad! You forgot your money!" All were a bit red-faced as they left that day, especially Papa.

During the winter, Roger would walk across the frozen Pasaic River to get to school. During the summer, the family would picnic together or go to a Bible camp on the Jersey shore.

World War II had been going on while Roger was in his earlier years of high school. When he was a senior, young men like Roger had major decisions to make related into which branch of the service they would enlist. He wasn't interested in being on a ship the whole time, so the navy was out. He also didn't want to be on foot carrying things as he walked, so that pretty much crossed the army off his list, except the army had an area that had an interesting job to offer a recent high school graduate called the army air corps.

CHAPTER 2

The Lord Brings Us Together

Then the Lord God said, It is not good for the man to be alone; I will make him a helper suitable for him.

—Genesis 2:18

The army air corps really caught Roger's eye and his heart. He would learn to fly, and for many years, that had been a dream of his. The thought of flying fighter planes really was one exciting turn of events for him, so he enlisted and waited to be called up. Sometimes he was disappointed that it took so long, but the wait was of a greater power than Uncle Sam.

In was in this interim period that he had some free time. His oldest brother, Earl, and his wife, Grace, moved from a church in New Jersey to pastor a church in Baltimore, Maryland. They got moved and settled, then invited family for a visit. Roger was one of the first family visitors. Even though Earl was eighteen years senior to Roger and more like an uncle than a brother, these men were very fond of each other. It was a good visit, and Roger enjoyed his nephews Brian and Brent. Earl and Grace had been married eight years before the boys were born, and Roger made a terrific babysitter.

The weekend brought some new life into Roger. His church in Totowa had lots of children but not many young people. On Sunday, Roger was excited and happy to see a Sunday school circle of young people his age. All seemed so friendly. He met one young lady, Mary, whom he walked home after church. It was a good friendship and lingered for a time.

It seems weekends had special events, and Roger found a train trip most satisfying. He became an active part of the Christian Endeavor in Forest Park Presbyterian Church. He especially liked one of the guys, Marvin Mayers, my brother. He liked the group, and the young people liked him. He was a very handsome addition to our youth group. Mary seemed content to have him walk her home.

Our group met on Sunday night one weekend, and Roger was there. Some of us girls were in the powder room upstairs and got to talking about the guys. "Don't you think Roger is adorable?" one girl said.

"Absolutely not," I said.

"He has beautiful eyes," another girl said.

He just didn't appeal to me, but each of the others thought he was the cat's meow.

Another said, "You just don't like guys."

I retorted that I had plans that didn't include boys. I was planning on going to the famous Wheaton College before heading to the mission field. That was foremost in my thinking. Wheaton was famous because it stood as the tower of Christian colleges, and I had my heart set on going there. However, my heart was broken as I had applied and had been rejected as I had not been in the top half of my high school class.

That summer after high school graduation, I was working as a secretary in my dad's office during the day and was attending a business college in the evenings. I also was vice president of the youth group at church. Because we had so many young men being called up to go to war, it seemed that every time we turned around, someone was leaving. We tried to have a party for each one. At this time, there was a party for George Hoffman, a quiet young man. His parents wanted the youth group to come to their home for a party for their son.

I had decided not to attend the party because of my work and school schedule. The phone rang, and a familiar voice asked me if I was going to George's party. I said I wasn't because of school. It was Roger, and he sounded disappointed, but I had no clue as to why he called. He said goodbye, and I went back to work.

My dad wanted to know what that was all about, and I told him. He felt very strongly that I should go to George's party. As a leader in the group, he felt I should be there to say goodbye. I tossed the idea around a bit and got back to my filing.

At closing time, Dad said, "Are you going to school tonight, or are you going home with me?" I had decided to go home with Dad. We had a good visit all the way home. I didn't usually get those visits because most nights I went home on the streetcar after school. The streetcar in those days was a pretty good way to transport a person from one side of Baltimore to the other.

After we arrived home, we were just getting seated at the dinner table when the phone rang. I answered and heard that familiar voice again. "I was just checking to see if you were coming to the party this evening," he said.

"Yes, I am," I replied.

"Can you bring your camera?" he asked.

When I got off the phone, the family wanted to know who had called. I told them it was Roger. Smiles went around the table. We had our blessing and ate.

Edna next door called to see if I was going to the party, and we took off soon after to get there on time. It was a good evening, and many of the youth group came. I was happy I didn't have to go to school. Mrs. Hoffman had gone to a lot of trouble to have a nice evening for her son.

It seemed everywhere I went, I had a shadow. I really didn't mind having the attention of a young man. I wondered what happened between him and Mary. When asked if he could walk Edna and myself home, I found myself saying, "Yes."

There were funny feelings inside of me as we walked along to my house. I didn't know what to make of his attention nor his trying to hold my hand as we walked. Edna later told me later she had thought all evening that he was interested in me, and I kept saying, "No, she was dreaming it all up."

Two weeks later asked me for a date. I was eighteen years old and had never been on a date before, but I said, "Yes. I guess that will be okay." I think my family was more excited than I, but I was excited, too. I looked forward to that evening with much anticipation and joy.

When Roger arrived at my door that night of our first date, I could feel the pangs of anticipation as I opened the door to ask him to come in. My heart stood still for those first few minutes. I still felt those pangs all those years later just thinking about it.

My dad asked him where we were going, and Roger replied that he thought he would take me to a theater to see a movie that had just come to town. Dad reached into his pocket and handed Roger the keys to his car. He encouraged us to be careful and for Roger to have me home before midnight.

Giving Roger the car keys was something of a miracle. I could see Mom was not so excited about us going to a movie but wished us well as we walked out to the car. Dad only used the car for work and going to church and the annual trip to Ohio to see my grandmothers.

We talked and talked and talked. Getting to know each other was really something special. We both could say at the end of the evening that it was a wonderful date. We enjoyed being together, and I really couldn't tell you anything about the movie.

His going into the army air corps was something he was excited about, and my going to the mission field made us both do some deep thinking. That first date brought up a lot of major decisions, so many questions. We knew we enjoyed being together. We also knew our dating was going to be long distance with letters going back and forth with phone calls in between. He told me later that he fell in love with me that night. It took me a bit longer, but I knew I missed him when the train pulled away that weekend taking him back to Totowa to await Uncle Sam's first notice.

Between March 28 and Easter that year, Roger decided to return to Baltimore for another visit. The office phone rang, and it was Roger asking if it was okay for him to visit me at the office. I was surprised by the call, for I thought he was in Totowa. But I was more surprised when he walked in the door a few minutes later. He had called from the corner store and wanted to surprise me. He did. My dad told me to take some time and go for a walk, so we did.

There was another time that Edna and I met Roger at the train station in Philadelphia, which was midway between Totowa and Baltimore. Edna had to open the family farmhouse for her folks. We had a wonderful day in Philadelphia. We did some sightseeing, listened to the organ at Wanamaker's Department Store; cleaned up the farm house for the family to be able to enjoy later; saw the Liberty Bell, Independence Hall, and the church tower, taking pictures of it all.

We went to a pharmacy that we were told served delicious sandwiches. Edna and I had a club sandwich, and Roger ordered a grape jelly, cream cheese, and peanut butter sandwich. We had ordered the most expensive sandwich on the menu, and he ordered the least expensive. Edna and I offered to pay for ours. Roger laughed and said, "This is my treat."

We had a good laugh, and we continued to enjoy the day.

Vending machines were relatively new in those days. Horn & Hardart was a neat place to have a bowl of soup for a quick meal. We put coins in a box, made our selection, and we were rewarded with a bowl of yummy soup.

After our early supper, we headed to the train station. Roger was off to Totowa, and we girls headed to Baltimore for a streetcar home. All of us were weary, but it had been a wonderful day. I wondered when we would be able to have a good time like that again.

Philadelphia held a lot of charm for us, and over the years, we enjoyed other visits there. We especially enjoyed that organ music and the restaurant meals on the top floor of the department store.

Time had a way of flying. After our first date, Roger received his notice from the military to be sworn in. That was on Easter Sunday in 1943. He was so excited when he called to tell me his news and then was sad when I told him that I had not been accepted into Wheaton College.

I found some beautiful blue stationery called "Calais blue" and bought my first of many boxes. Letters became an almost-daily ritual for me. Roger loved hearing from me, and I loved hearing from him.

Roger had caught a train out of Newark, New Jersey, after he was sworn in, but he didn't know where he was going for basic training. His brother Earl and I thought the train would go through Baltimore so that Sunday after church, we went to the train station to check on trains, up one line to the next, looking in all the windows to see if we could see Roger.

I had a package of homemade cookies, and Earl had a package for him too, and although we spent several hours looking in train windows, we did not see him and headed home very disappointed.

Roger was in the army air corps, going to war overseas, and I was at home working in my dad's office equipment company. Lots of questions were going through our minds. We communicated the best we could with almost-daily letters going back and forth. We had questions about what we wanted to do with our lives. How could we rectify Roger being a pilot and the feeling in my heart that God wanted me to go to the mission field? He had told me once that he would go and be a repairman while I talked to the people about Jesus.

At that time, Borneo was much on my heart, although I was really more interested in Borneo for the adventure. I knew that I would be inland ten days, so I decided I needed to be a pilot. I needed some nurse's training, so nursing school also was a goal. And I needed to go to a Christian college for missionary training. Roger was willing to go, but it wasn't a call from God. He was going just to be with me.

The summer of 1943 had lots of decision discussions going back and forth for both of us. He was making new friends in Texas while learning to be a pilot. He wanted to see me, but there was no way for us to visit in person. The Calais blue paper kept flowing every day. We really were in love but needed some guidance as we thought about "after the war." We managed to keep busy and as happy as we could under the circumstances.

CHAPTER 3

A Year at Wheaton College

And Jesus said to them, "Follow me and I will
make you become fishers of men."

—Mark 1:17

Forest Park Presbyterian Church opened the door for some of us young people to attend a week of conference in August 1943 at Keswick, New Jersey. I had heard Dr. V. Raymond Edman, president of Wheaton College, was going to be at Keswick that summer. Dad and Mom said they would take us up there to Toms River if any of us wanted to go. Dad enjoyed trips like that. Mary, Ruth, and I were elected to go.

It was a good week, and it brought some amazing turn of events. Bible study was good with Dr. Edman teaching during the week, and it made me want to go to Wheaton all the more.

The very first afternoon, Dr. Edman stopped me and asked if I would like to have devotions with him at 5:00 a.m. the next morning. He told me he liked to row out to the middle of the lake and study God's Word without interruptions and noise. I jumped at the idea. I wanted to know this man. I don't think anything could have kept me from getting up and meeting him at the dock.

We got into a small boat, and I rowed us out to the middle of the lake. He talked about Jesus as though He was a real person. I was amazed at his love for Jesus. I knew I didn't have that relationship at that time. I met Dr. Edman at the dock each morning at 5:00 a.m. It was a wonderful way to start the day.

I could hardly share how much that week meant to me as I wrote to Roger, and more Calais blue passed through the mail than ever. I wanted him to know everything, especially the night of the missionary speaker, Dr. Ivan Albutt. He was so excited about the work he was doing in the jungles of Indonesia. He made it sound like they were out of this world—so beautiful.

One night, I had my lap full of books I had purchased from the sale rack. My Bible and the books were heavy. Dr. Albutt gave the invitation, and I knew I needed to go forward. A song was humming through the music hall.

> I'll go where you want me to go dear Lord,
> I'll be what you want me to be.
> I'll say what you want me to say Lord,
> I'll go where you want me to go.

I couldn't get that song out of my head, and at that moment of thinking, Dr. Edman took the books off my lap. It was as if a huge burden was lifted as I went forward to join with other young people, who also were responding to the call of the Lord's voice to be willing to go and serve Him overseas.

The message reaffirmed my desire to go to the mission field. After Saturday morning devotions, Dr. Edman and I hurried to the dining room. After breakfast, someone called my name and handed me a telegram. I ripped it open, thinking that my dad would be late in picking me up, but as I read, tears came to my eyes.

I saw the Lord Jesus at work as I read through the telegram that had come from Wheaton College. I nearly flipped as I became so excited. I had been accepted! My parents too were excited as I shared the news with them. Room had been made for me at Wheaton in "East Gate" for September 7.

I shared the news with Dr. Edman, who smiled and said, "See you in a few weeks" at Wheaton. The twinkle in his eye let me know he was the instrument God used to get me there.

Roger was excited about my time at Keswick and wanted to hear more about my plans to be a missionary. He was still in Texas flying. And flying was something, it seemed, he would rather do than eat. Roger told me in one letter that his sergeant had instructed the fellows if they got lost, to follow the highways. Roger wrote he did get lost one time. He did follow the highways to get back to his base, but he followed the wrong highways and ended up at another base. His commanding officer had to go get him and fly back to his base. Roger was embarrassed, but he learned his lesson. He was a determined young man.

I had about two and a half weeks to have things ready for college, and that time really flew by. What to take or not to take was on my mind. Wheaton had very cold winters. After I decided what to take to college, my steamer trunk and suitcases were packed and taken from my house to the train station, put on a train, and taken to Wheaton. It was exciting to know that I would be going to college. It also was my first time away from home. I was really homesick that year at Wheaton. I know my parent's phone bill must have doubled.

On September 19, 1943, there were special meetings in the gym with speaker Joe Hankins. The freshmen didn't know what to expect, but all six hundred students were required to attend the meetings. I heard so many things abfout the "Christian life" that I had never heard before. It boggled my mind. I was a girl who had grown up in a very strict Presbyterian home. Everything I wanted to do had a "no-no" attached to it—no dancing, no swearing, no movies, no drinking—and the list went on and on.

This man talked about a life in Jesus Christ, and it was wonderful. His first message was about having two birthdays and how important that was. I knew when I was born, but when was the second birthday? I had one in May, but what did he mean by two?

I listened with all my heart. I didn't have two birthdays. I began to see that my heart was black and dirty. I thought of the many things I had done wrong, and when he said, "Young lady, young man, do you really know who Jesus is?" I could say through my tears, "No," and when the invitation was given, I found myself stumbling to the prayer room and fell on my knees. Someone else slumped down beside me. I turned to see Dr. Edman, the president of Wheaton College, his eyes wet with tears. He told me he had been praying for this moment.

He spoke softly to me and said, "Meg, I knew at Keswick that you had good head knowledge of the Lord Jesus but that you didn't know Him personally. What do you want to do about it?"

I said through my tears, "I want to ask Jesus into my heart."

He explained the plan of salvation. I prayed and asked Jesus to forgive my sins, and He came into my heart. And then Dr. Edman prayed. Romans 10:9–10 became very real to me that evening. Inside, I knew I was a new person.

> That if you confess with your mouth Jesus as Lord, and believe in your heart that God raised Him from the dead, you will be saved; for with the heart man believes, resulting in righteousness, and with the mouth he confesses, resulting in salvation.

The following morning, after my decision to walk with Jesus, Dr. Edman called my name with many other names to see him after chapel. It was at that session the he asked us to meet with him each Tuesday after chapel. What is called discipleship today took place the rest of the school year.

What a thrill it was to meet with the president each Tuesday. God and His Word took on a real meaning to me. One thing I knew was that God was calling me to be a missionary. I was going to trust Him to see me through to His place of service. Going to the mission field was not just an adventure; I knew God had special plans for me. I had a longing to share Jesus with everyone I knew.

Then I knew why I was at Keswick with Dr. Edman that August and why I received the telegram letting me know I would be going to Wheaton. He knew I didn't know the Lord but that I had a burden to serve somewhere and that I was willing to go.

I wrote everything that had transpired in me to Roger, and it had a new ring to it. I no longer was to be a missionary for the adventure and excitement; I was going to be a missionary because I wanted to see people come to Jesus. His reply was that he was so happy for me and was praying that he would have the same assurance. The more letters were written, the more we grew to know about each other. He was a wonderful man. I was falling more and more in love with him each day and he with me.

He looked for my letters each day, and I looked for his too, but we had mixed emotions about our future. Everything I learned, I shared on Calais blue paper, and he began to be more and more open to the Word of God.

Wheaton really was God's choice for me for the 1943–44 school year, but it was short-lived. After one of our Tuesday study sessions, Dr. Edman had some papers for me to read. They were application forms for Columbia Bible College in South Carolina. I read through them and then Dr. Edman said, "Meg. This is where you need to go to get the training you need to go to the mission field."

At first I was crushed, but as we talked, I began to understand what he was saying. My year at Wheaton was a good one and taught me so many things about the Christian life—I was alive—but the year was coming to an end in May 1944.

I was accepted to CBC, and I rejoiced at how the Lord took care of me. It was another step in my walk with the Lord, and I knew then, as I learned over and over, things don't just "happen." They are planned by God's own hand.

Roger had wanted me to fly to Texas to see him get his wings at flight school graduation, but when I asked my parents, Dad told me Mother was ill and I needed to come home. I wanted to go to Texas so badly, especially knowing that Roger's parents were going to be there. I obeyed my dad and returned to Baltimore when school was out, but my heart was in Texas.

In August 1944, we had a really big date coming up just about a year after we started dating. Roger wanted me to come to a family reunion in Connecticut. Roger's aunt Matt and uncle Mally were house sitters for several wealthy people's vacation homes in Connecticut, and the family was always invited, with the owner's consent, to come for the weekend and enjoy the place, too. Earl and

Grace were going, and Earl said I could drive there with them and the boys.

Roger and I were so happy to see each other. The vacation home was huge; there were bedrooms everywhere. Each family had a place to call their own. It was near the ocean, and the view from nearly every window was ocean filled. What a place to spend that weekend together.

The family loved playing on the beach, throwing balls, and making sand castles and towers. Everything was new to me. Going swimming in the ocean was a challenge for me because I was not crazy about it. A lot of laughing and squealing was going on. The little kids were having such fun. In fact, we all were.

Saturday evening after supper, Roger asked me to go for a walk on the beach. We walked down to the seawall to sit on it and watch the sunset. What a gorgeous sight. I still recall that evening as we talked and talked about the day and our lives.

We had made plans to go to New York City after we had returned to his parent's home in Totowa. He asked if there was something special I wanted to see, and I told him no. He told me he wanted to get me something special, a ring. He took me in his arms and asked me to marry him. I did a silly little thing and laughed. He never let me live down that moment.

Getting engaged seemed so foreign to me, but in my heart, I really wanted to say yes, and I did. Our kiss sealed the precious moment. I think I walked on air the rest of the reunion. We also decided that we would not marry if Roger were not called to serve. God had other plans that He was working out, and we were watching it all fall into place.

We also decided to keep this event a secret until I could tell my folks after we got home. Roger and I rode back to Baltimore with Earl and Grace.

When we told my mom and dad the news, my dad gave Roger a warm handshake, and when he took Roger to the train station to return to the base, he said to Roger, "Well, son, welcome to the family." Mom was a bit more reserved as I recall, but she did come around in time, and he knew she loved him.

Our day in New York City was wonderful. Roger was so handsome in his army air corps pink shirt/green uniform with the shining pilot's wings. I loved to see the other servicemen salute my officer-fiancé.

CHAPTER 4

Off to Japan, the First Time

When you go to war in your land against the adversary who attacks you, then you shall sound an alarm with trumpets, that you may be remembered before the Lord your God, and be saved from your enemies.

—Numbers 10:9

Roger's trip in a P-47 heading to the South Pacific became a reality, and I was going to South Carolina to attend Columbia Bible College just as Dr. Edman had encouraged me to do in April 1944. Letters from Roger became fewer and fewer apart. Not knowing where he was proved difficult for me. I found out later that it also was tough on him, too, for he didn't receive my letters regularly, either. When he did, it was a pile of Calais blue that was handed to him. It was normal for servicemen not to receive mail regularly because they often were moving around. I kept on writing.

I was one of only two girls at CBC who was engaged. My ten-by-twelve picture of Roger in his uniform was often used in school programs, so everyone knew him by his picture and his name. Those days were so hard. I wanted to talk with him but could not. We both struggled, but compared to the reality of war in which he was living, my life at CBC was so carefree.

CBC had some rules to obey that were pretty rigid for all the students, mostly girls at that time. There were a few underage boys and some boys classified as 4-F, unfit for military duty, because of physical problems, and forty or so who were studying to become pastors. School activities centered around the piano for hymn sing-alongs in the sunroom and picnics in Columbia City Park, where we also played baseball.

One of the rules, no matter what, was that girls had to wear silk stockings—baggy silk stockings. They weren't exactly choice things to wear at a picnic and definitely not for playing baseball. My team was up to bat with the bases loaded. I wanted to hit a home run so badly. I hit the ball, rounded first, and slid into second while two teammates crossed the plate. My classmate Robertson McQuilkin was waiting for the ball. As I slid into second, my garter belt gave way, leaving me standing there with baggy silk stockings down around my ankles, safe but so embarrassed.

Robertson held his coat around me so that I could get fastened again, and the game continued. I don't remember who won the game that day, but it was the last time we were required to wear stockings to the park. The board was meeting, and Robertson told his dad that he had something to tell the board. He shared the story, and the men and women of the board voted to allow girls to wear anklets instead of stockings for the next picnic. That was a first in changing the rules at the college. We girls were very happy.

Roger's life of flying in the Pacific was of a different nature, to say the least. He didn't enjoy the war but did enjoy the flying. Flying, eating, sleeping, and writing a few sentences on a piece of paper to his family and to me was his daily routine. He had a mindset that he was going to see all that he could and enjoy it in spite of the war. He loved meeting people in the lands where he was stationed.

Roger moved from one island to the next following General MacArthur's command. I couldn't begin to tell you where his P-47 took him. He was happy in the little plane he had named "Little Eva" after his mother, and he loved me. His letters were screened by army regulations, and he couldn't write where he was or what he was doing. But he could write, "I love you," and that permeated his letters. Verses he had read that meant something to him also filled a page or so. We were eager for the war to be over with, but then, so was everyone else.

He was now nineteen years old, a fighter pilot in the war in many areas of the Pacific. His parents never expected him to come home. The war was fierce. I lived in my little world in the dorm; he lived in a dangerous world all around the Far East.

Studying God's Word was great, refreshing as our professors made the Bible come live. The Christian walk became so real. We were being challenged in chapel by missionaries from around the world—China, Africa, India, South Africa—these men and women had pioneered and seen harvest come as nationals came to know the Lord.

Borneo still kept coming to my mind, and I began to question Roger's call to go. We had gotten engaged with the understanding that when the war was over, if he didn't have the call, our engagement was over. Sometimes, there would be a pang of feelings that I should stop writing. Sometimes, I wrote "Dear John" letters, and my roommate Ann would be so frustrated with me. She never let me send the "Dear John" letters I had written. She would say, "You love him. God knows that. He'll come around."

At the same time God was working on me, He too was working on Roger. One letter that came after that first year he was overseas was probably the most exciting I had received. He always started out his letters with "My Dearest Wife 2B."

He went on, "You will be happy to know that tonight, I surrendered my heart to Jesus. I know He wants me as well as you to serve Him."

I read that letter over and over and over. The girls had a praise and prayer meeting that evening. I was so excited and happy.

> And when I came to you, brethren, I did not
> come with superiority of speech or of wisdom,
> proclaiming to you the testimony of God. For I
> determined to know nothing among you except
> Jesus Christ, and Him crucified. And I was

with you in weakness and in fear and in much trembling, and my message and my preaching were not in persuasive words of wisdom, but in demonstration of the Spirit and of power, so that your faith should not rest on the wisdom of men, but on the power of God. (1 Corinthians 2:1–5)

For Roger, this decision was tough. He loved flying, not fighting and war. But he knew in his heart that God had spoken to his heart through a message about full surrender. That was what World War II was about—full surrender of the enemy. The chaplain spoke about this, and when Roger left the mortuary building where Christian services were being held for soldiers in Manila, Philippines, the voice was saying to him, "Why not surrender?" and he did to God. He had full assurance of his salvation. There were many very happy people as the news traveled.

We knew God had called us to serve Him. Now came the "where." Borneo still was on my heart. I had developed a skin problem with formaldehyde in a science lab. It kept getting worse, which put serious doubt on my becoming a nurse. My first ride in a small plane made me realize that being a pilot was not my cup of tea. So little by little, I could see God closing some doors and opening others.

CHAPTER 5

Christian Service: Hitting the Streets

The wages of sin is death, but the free gift of God
is eternal life in Christ Jesus our Lord.

—Romans 6:23

M r. Sells, our Bible teacher, and Dr. McQuilkin were excellent teachers and with their superior teaching helped us to grow in our faith and walk with Jesus. Dr. McQuilkin had been a missionary volunteer. He and his wife were off to Africa in 1923 when they loaded their baggage on board ship in New York City. They went back to their hotel room and in the morning arrived at the dock to find the ship was gone. Much to their surprise among the hubbub at the dock, they found the ship had sunk.

Several women were there to see the McQuilkins leave and offered their sorrow with them, but as they stood there on the dock, someone said something like, "Now you can go back to Columbia, South Carolina, and start a Bible college."

That was a big change in plans, but all had peace that this was God's will, and over the next months, Columbia Bible College grew in hearts and minds. It opened with some young people who wanted to serve the Lord overseas. What a switch in plans! But they learned that God didn't make mistakes. The old hotel in Columbia, with its finial in the sky, became a place and home for many students who grew in their desire to serve God.

Over the years, I was impressed with Dr. and Mrs. McQuilkin's fervor to see young people go forth to serve the Lord. All six of their children were called of God to various areas of the world. I will never forget the joy there was sitting under their teaching.

Mr. and Mrs. Sells were vibrant in making God's Word come alive. Mrs. Sells taught classes on object lessons and broke down Bible lessons that could be taught to children. I loved being in her class. Mr. Sells' review of the Old Testament and New Testament really brought the Bible alive in our hearts. He was a wonderful man of the Word. Just as God was with the children of Israel in the Old Testament, we found the same God with us all the time, too.

Mr. Hehl taught us how to memorize and use God's Word and make it relevant to our day-to-day living. We also were required to go out on the streets and witness for Christ each week. We also went to the South Carolina State Fair and had a CBC booth that we students staffed, and we shared Jesus with everyone we met along the way.

I lived in the dorm with my roommate Ann. She was good for me. Mr. Hehl had our class go out two by two and stop people on the street and share the plan of salvation with them. That was so difficult but so rewarding too. On our first day, we encountered a heavyset black woman with a beautiful smile walking toward us. Ann volunteered me to talk, and she could pray.

I stopped this smiling lady and said we were from the Bible college and asked if she knew Jesus. Smiling even more, she said, "I sure do," and explained how she asked Him into her heart. She went on and told us her husband John did, too. John happened to be the elevator man in our dorm. Mr. Hehl used to quote, "The wages of sin is death," to John up the elevator and down the elevator, in the halls and in the dining room. Whenever he was near John, that was all he would say.

Finally, John said, "Mr. Hehl, sir, but isn't there any more to that verse?" When he found out there was—"but the free gift from God is eternal life in Christ Jesus our Lord"—he asked, "Can't I ask Jesus into my heart?"

Mr. Hehl then led him to Jesus.

The lady said, "Oh, Missy, that was a happy day for me," and she went her way, and Ann and I headed back to college. We enjoyed our sidewalk evangelism when we could share Jesus with others.

My Christian service one semester was teaching a day Bible class in a black home. I loved those little children and was so excited when one and then another came to Jesus.

Another semester, my Christian service was teaching the Bible to ghetto kids in the city park in Columbia. Freshmen and sophomores were told all they were to do the first week was to watch, but they were short of teachers, and I was asked to teach. I didn't have a lesson planned, but I quickly asked Jesus what to do and say, and He said, "Use the wordless book."

I had seen my mother use that book in many Child Evangelism Fellowship classes.

Black—your heart's sin—"For all have sinned and fall short of the glory of God" (Romans 3:23).

Red—Jesus's blood—"For the wages of sin is death, but the free gift of God is eternal life in Christ Jesus our Lord" (Romans 6:23).

White—your clean heart—"In the exercise of His will He brought us forth by the word of truth, so that we would be kind of first fruits among His creatures" (James 1:18).

Gold—heaven finally is your home—"but if we walk in the light as He Himself is in the light, we have fellowship with one another, and the blood of Jesus His Son cleanses us from all sin. If we confess our sins, He is faithful and righteous to forgive us our sins and cleanse us from all unrighteousness" (1 John 1:7, 9).

Green—grow like a tree, strong and firm—"He said to me, It is done. I am the Alpha, and the Omega, the beginning, and the end. I will give to the one who thirsts from the spring of water of life without cost. But for the cowardly and unbelieving and abominable and murderers and immoral persons and sorcerers and idolaters and all liars, their part will be in the lake that burns with fire and brimstone" (Revelation 21:6–7).

Blue—do not be troubled—"Sanctify Christ as Lord in your hearts, always being ready to make a defense to everyone who asks you to give an account for the hope that is in you, yet, with gentleness and reverence" (1 Peter 3:15).

The children loved looking for verses, and at the end of the class, a dirty-faced little girl snuggled up to me and said she wanted to ask Jesus into her heart. That was a thrill to be sure. I loved those girls.

CHAPTER 6

God Was at Work, Even in War

For where two or three have gathered together in
My name, I am there in their midst.

—Matthew 18:20

In her book *Through Open Doors: A History of SEND International*, Mildred M. Morehouse, a forty-five-year missionary with FEGC/SEND International in Japan, described the beginnings of the GI Gospel Hour in New Guinea, the Philippines, and then Japan. Men and women involved in the GI Gospel Hour were some of the early pioneers of the Far Eastern Gospel Crusade that later became SEND International.

During World War II, wherever American GIs were stationed, Christians somehow managed to find each other. They would notice a fellow soldier who didn't use foul language or one who took time to bow his head before eating. These Christian men and women found time to gather for personal prayer and fellowship. In time, at Milne Bay, New Guinea, these informal gatherings of GIs were encouraged and legitimized before military authorities by the cooperation of chaplains.

Other soldiers heard about the gatherings by word of mouth and joined them. New faces appeared almost nightly, soon crowding out the tent where meetings had been held. The GIs petitioned for a site on base for their meetings. They received permission, but there were no materials with which to build. They ended up building a twenty-foot-by-thirty-foot chapel using lumber from crates used to ship supplies to the American command. As word got out, other materials needed for construction were donated. Other items, such as seating, were salvaged from wrecked trucks.

Within two weeks, the chapel was completed and dedicated in November 1943. As numbers grew, the chapel was expanded twice until it could seat two hundred.

American forces took Hollandia on the North Central coast of New Guinea in April 1944. Personnel and materiel was transferred from Milne Bay to Hollandia. The Christian GIs built another chapel there, and the first rally was held in February 1945. Attendance grew from about seventy-five to three hundred by mid-March.

With the preaching of the familiar gospel and the energetic singing of songs similar to the Youth for Christ meetings back home, the gatherings became a rallying point for Christian GIs. Chaplain Leon Hawley's Bible studies were a main attraction, and through these rallies and the Bible studies, many found Christ and were grounded in their faith.

After American forces returned to liberate the Philippines in 1945, Christian GIs of many different denominations still gathered to share and to hear the gospel. Once radio stations returned to the airwaves, airtime was purchased to broadcast the meetings GIs had been attending. It was called the GI Gospel Hour and was broadcast on Saturday nights. The meetings were held to full audiences, often with others sitting in windows or listening outdoors.

The GI Gospel Hour was Roger's favorite place to go on Saturdays. Good music, good messages from God's Word, and bonding with other Christians was a joy he never would forget. He wanted to take me to the Philippines so very much, but that was a few years down the road.

Mildred Morehouse described when American forces moved on to Japan, the GI Gospel Hour moved with them. The first GI Gospel Hour meeting in Japan was held in November 1945 at the Ginza Methodist Church in downtown Tokyo. The roof had a bomb hole in it, and the windows had been blown out, along with other damage, but the pastor was willing for the GIs to use the building. More than two hundred attended that first night. The hole in the roof and broken-out windows allowed the fervent singing of the GIs to be heard in neighborhoods around the church. The GI Gospel Hour also moved to Yokohama.

Morehouse wrote, "Roger Fox, stationed at Atsugi Air Base, brought truckloads of GIs to the Gospel Hour in Yokohama."

Roger also was one of a group of men who got Youth for Christ meetings going at Atsugi to reach Japanese youth as well. Between one thousand and two thousand young Japanese people attended the first ever Youth for Christ meeting for Japanese youth.

* * * * *

Roger met a fellow named Dub Jackson in Atsugi. He was a Christian Southern Baptist from Texas. They became fast friends even though Dub really liked playing his cornet at all hours. Roger ended up in Dub's barracks along with several other Christian GIs.

Dub and Roger were introduced to five missionary women who had stayed in Japan during the war, including Miss Mabel Frances and her sister Mrs. Anne Dievendorf, who was an English teacher who had tutored Emperor Hirohito in his English. She was a Christian and shared her faith with the emperor.

One of those women had a burden for children who had been orphaned, and she wanted to start an orphanage. It became a reality for ten to twelve children in an old home with Honichi san, a Japanese Christian *obasan* (grandmother) who loved them and took care of them. Roger and Dub would take food to the orphanage when they could. Food was scarce at the time, and the women and children loved having something different from time to time.

Roger and Dub scrounged mattresses, old clothes, and wool blankets and took them to the missionaries to use to make clothing. Even though some of the wool clothing caused the children to itch, they were happy to be warm.

One time, Roger and another of his cohorts Bob Millar had an opportunity to borrow a jeep and drive to Yonezawa, about two hundred miles north of Tokyo, where there was a silk center. They were away for several days but made sure there was food for all five missionaries and the dozen or so children in the orphanage. Roger was learning that the Lord had wonderful ways of taking care of him during those days.

The short trip to Yonezawa was fabulous and turned into twelve days. Roads were not so good with ruts and potholes. The rickety old jeep had a lot to be desired, but they bounced along the rut-filled roads to buy some silk. They found several natural hot springs, tried their hand at snow skiing, and yes, they did buy a quantity of silk.

Roger and Bob received permission to leave the base and go to Yonezawa as long as they brought silk back for their commanding officers, which they did. Roger also found several large pieces of silk for my wedding dress, or so he thought. They believed they had purchased enough silk to make what was necessary, but when we opened the packages he had shipped home, we found it was enough silk to make an *obi*, a sash for a kimono, and not enough material at all to make a dress.

As it turned out, creative Mama Fox made bed jackets for all the girls in the family and then hankies with what was left over. I don't know anyone else who had pure silk bed jackets and hankies, but we all did. They were pretty too, with pink, yellow, and green flowers embroidered on them.

Besides his regular army air force duties, he also was deeply involved with the GI Gospel Hour in Tokyo and Yokohama, the orphanage, teaching English to Japanese youngsters, Youth for Christ in Atsugi, and also the airbase Servicemen for Christ. God was working in him and through him even before we went to the mission field.

Roger's time in Occupied Japan really planted seeds in his heart, including meeting the missionaries who were interned during the war. Seeing their love for the Japanese children opened his heart to the needs of that country for spiritual food in each heart. He loved the children who unfortunately had been orphaned by the war. He loved the Japanese he met wherever he went. He felt awful when he saw that food was scarce and clothing not plentiful to keep them warm. He had a desire to return to share the gospel with those he met. He wrote once, asking if my dad, who was on the board of the Pocket Testament League, would be able to have some Bibles printed in Japanese and shipped over because there was such a hunger for the Word of God. He loved Japan as a country and conveyed that to me in his letters.

General MacArthur wanted missionaries for Japan to come and replace guns with Bibles. That became Roger's burden too as the next years came and went. He planned to come home for "temporary duty" with the thought that he would be going back after he graduated from college. His enthusiasm rubbed off on me, and I too began to pray that we could go there to work. Borneo never left my thoughts, but in time, I knew in my heart that it was not God's place for me.[1]

---

[1] Mildred. M. Morehouse; Through Open Doors, a History of SEND International; published by SEND International; Detroit, MI; pages 3–45

CHAPTER 7

Wedding Bells

So husbands ought to love their own wives as their own bodies. He who loves his wife loves himself; for no one ever hated his own flesh, but nourishes and cherishes it, just as Christ also does for the church, because we are members of His body.

—Ephesians 5:28–30

Many weeks would pass, and I heard nothing from him. His parents "knew" he had been killed, but I had it in my heart that he was busy and would write when he could. The longer that no word came, I too started to grow concerned as well.

One evening, the telephone girl on the third floor came to my room to tell me I had a call from Washington. It didn't take long for me to sprint to the top floor, thinking it was a call from my dad who often had trips to Washington, DC, for the Simplex Time Recorder Company. With that thought in mind, I said, "Hi, Dad!"

The voice on the other end said, "Hi, honey. I'm home!"

Roger was in Seattle, Washington, not Washington, DC. I screamed and screamed and screamed. I was told that every girl on the dorm was in the hall, waiting to find out what happened. When I finally quieted down, Roger said, "I'll be at CBC next week. I'm getting discharged in Newark and going to my folks, then I will catch a train to Columbia that following Monday."

I was so excited; I could hardly wait to tell everyone.

When I got to the snack bar that evening, everyone there knew my lieutenant was home from the war and would be in Columbia next week. Roger's brother Earl wanted him to attend Marysville College, a very Presbyterian college. He thought about it, but in the end, Roger made it plain that he was going to Columbia Bible College. That was settled when he was accepted. He had some credits from the University of Alabama when he was studying to be a pilot, and he was excited about going to CBC.

Everyone welcomed Roger so warmly. Almost immediately upon arrival, he wanted to set our wedding date. That meant I had to get permission from Mrs. Walker, our dean of students. Roger's application was just one of the many from servicemen applying to college. Some felt like Roger did do "temporary duty" in college and get back overseas with the Word of God and not guns and ammunition.

We selected June 22, 1946 for our wedding. It was now April 1946, and I had the semester to finish. While we shared thoughts about our wedding through letters, we really didn't have the luxury of having months for planning.

God's timing was perfect. Upon arriving home, our first task was to order flowers, the cake, and secure a caterer in that order. My dress and bridesmaids' dresses were next on the to-do list. Shopping in Baltimore went well. My dress was beautiful white satin and on sale. I was thrilled. Bridesmaids' dresses—three of the same color and a maid of honor—were not as easy to find. However, we did find four dresses alike in design, although different in colors, but perfect sizes for the girls.

Brown jackets with white slacks were the order of the day for the guys. Everything fit together. It was wonderful and reassuring how everything fell into place. Finally, June 22 arrived.

The wedding was at Forest Park Presbyterian Church in Baltimore. Roger's brother Earl officiated. My roommate, Ann, was my maid of honor, along with my sister, Alice Kay, and my good friends, Mary Wills and Peggy Fountain, as maids of honor.

Roger's brother Stanley was his best man, along with my brother Marvin, Bill Vogl, Bob Wills, and Paul Wonders as groomsmen.

We girls had prayer together, and after each girl walked down the aisle, it was time for Dad to walk me toward Roger at the front of the church.

Dad was suffering from back problems and was stooped because the pain was so bad. He told me he was happy I was marrying Roger and felt I had a wonderful husband. As we walked down the aisle, I was so happy to see my sweetheart waiting for me.

When Earl asked if anyone had caused that this couple not be married, Roger told me later he was waiting for his eighteen-month-old nephew to say, "I do!" Roger's brother-in-law, Louis, had primed the pump by asking Craig if he wanted ice cream at the question moment. But all went well.

Betty Banks played the organ, Peggy sang "Living for Jesus," and Roger's brother Irving sang "The Lord's Prayer." It was a beautiful wedding and a real family affair.

Our first gift was from Papa and Mama Fox—a beautiful hand-cut sugar and creamer that had been a gift at their wedding. I felt so honored that they wanted us to have it. The catered supper was to be in my parent's backyard. Their garden was lovely for the occasion.

In those days, friends of the bride and groom often would play pranks on the newlyweds, but Roger had made a plan. He had asked Dad if Marvin could take us to the train station, and Dad said sure. After the festivities, Roger had Marvin get in the back seat of Dad's car, and then told me to get out when he told me and follow him. Roger drove Dad's car up the alley, and on cue, we both got out and raced to the front of the house where Earl was waiting to take us to town. Roger got there first and opened the door as I was running across the street. Bob Wills was coming, having missed the trip up the alley. He nearly ran me over as I crossed but stopped short. Earl backed up the entire length of the street and headed for town.

About that time, Roger said, "Earl! My camera is on the fireplace." So we detoured, and Roger left us parked, engine running, at a corner lot while he ran to get the camera. It didn't take long, and Earl took off again with Brian and Brent in the front seat beside him.

When we got to town, Roger asked Earl to stop and told me to get out with him. We grabbed our bags and Roger hailed a cab to take us to the Southern Hotel in Baltimore not too far from the shore. We could smell the spices from the McCormick Spice Company, and we darted into the hotel. A porter took our bags and escorted us to a lovely room.

The door to the room was closed, but the door to my heart was open as we sat embraced. We noticed it still was daylight and decided taking a walk would be fun. We had not had any followers from the wedding, so hand in hand we went down the stairs and out the front doors of the hotel. It was a lovely evening. We laughed at how well we had successfully dodged the others from the wedding and kept our honeymoon destination a secret. We were catching a train to Newark the next morning, where Papa Fox's car was hidden.

It was on the walk that holding hands came to have meaning. He would squeeze my hand three times and told me he was saying, "I love you." That show of affection was always special throughout our lives together.

It was a wonderful walk, a beautiful evening, and as we retraced our steps about to go back into the hotel, some cars went by with very noisy, happy young people calling out, "Goodnight, Margaret and Roger." Lillian, Peggy, Ann, Marvin, Jim, Bob, Mary, Ruth, Bill, etc. had found us after a jaunt to the train station. It was a fun time, and we were grateful for our friends.

We got back to our room and decided to call Grace, Earl's wife. She had been taken to a tuberculosis hospital, and had missed our wedding. We had told her we would call, and she was waiting for that time. She was so happy to hear about our day but sad that she missed it all. She laughed with us that our family and friends had found us after we "escaped." I'm sure she and Earl had some good laughs the next day.

That first evening as husband and wife is one I shall never forget, and that first night will always be ours. I was happy I had kept myself for him and our first time together. We were now husband and wife and very much in love.

The next morning, we were packed, had breakfast, and caught a cab to the train station. We boarded the train to Newark and arrived there a couple of hours later. We found Papa's Chevy and headed for the Catskill Mountains, where we were to spend a week.

Each day had some special memories—walking down behind the church, looking at wildflowers, lying in the lush grass near the reservoir, and eating a picnic lunch. And we had so much to talk about. We had been apart for two full years. We had written many letters to each other, but we still needed to catch up about each other, to fill in the blanks during those two years. We borrowed bicycles and had a wonderful time sightseeing in that little town. I was one scared kitten at the beginning of the week but purred more and more, growing together in love. We enjoyed our time so much at cousin Ruby's farm, where she and her husband lived. We loaded the tractor from the field and tossed hay in the racks in the barn.

Praying together, reading God's Word together, loving together, eating at the kitchen table—nothing fancy, just taking the time to get to know each other and love each other more. It was a honeymoon of a lifetime, for which I praised God every year. The week passed too quickly, and it was time to say goodbye to family and new friends.

Driving back to Baltimore was the first of many such trips. We arrived back at my folk's home welcomed with hugs from everyone. Roger really felt part of the family. My bedroom became our bedroom from then on. There was only one bathroom that was shared by my mom and dad, Marvin, and Alice. There was some jostling, but we all did well in sharing.

Several days later after more picture taking and fun gatherings, we were packed and headed for Totowa. The rest of the summer, we were going to be babysitting Brian and Brent at Mama and Papa Fox's house. Grace still was suffering from tuberculosis, and the doctors were not sure what they were going to do next.

Even though the house was small, our room had two cribs and a double bed. That was our home until we left for college in the fall. Roger's sister Winnie, her husband Louis, and their children Patricia, Lois, and Craig had another bedroom. The five children, aged one and a half up to age eight, loved being together and played well while the adults had other chores to keep them occupied. Winnie and Louie were with Mama and Papa until the house they were building was finished, although there was never a promise when it would be completed.

I recall one night a very loud fire alarm went off. I heard the alarm first, but Roger had been a volunteer fireman while in high school. I knew he was up and dressed and away as Brent called, "Auntie Meg! Are you still there?" Then Brian climbed into bed with me.

Both boys snuggled up next to me. I had to reassure both boys that all was well. When Roger returned, they hugged and hugged him. We all hoped there would not be many nights like that; however, there were more.

Mama was fastidious about cleaning bedrooms in the morning. All had to be in order, and for the most part, they were. One morning, we arrived at the table starved as always, with two little starving boys in tow. While we were eating, Mama disappeared. The next thing I knew, I realized my engagement ring was off my left hand. I went flying upstairs and found all the bedding being aired outside held by closed windows. My heart sank and realized Roger was standing right behind me.

"Honey, what's wrong?" he asked.

I showed him my finger with the lone wedding band. We both knew it had to be out the window when those sheets had been shaken. Outside the window was an empty grassy lot choked with weeds and my beautiful engagement ring somewhere on the ground. But where?

Roger got the troops together. Papa had gone to work. With five children, two sisters-in-law, and Mama, there was work to do. Winnie got the dishes in order, and Mama had wash to do. Roger directed traffic. Each child knew what to look for and went up and down through the grass and weeds. What seemed like hours was brought to a close as someone squealed, "Uncle Roger! Aunt Meg! We found it!" And sure enough there was my lovely ring. Roger quickly put it back on my finger, and we had it resized shortly thereafter so it wouldn't fall off again. The kids and us sure were happy to have found it. We decided it was our first miracle. So much happy hugging took place before the children headed out to play.

Every once in a while, Earl would come and visit with the boys for a day or so. On one trip, his news was not so great. Grace wasn't getting any better. It was suggested to Earl that he take her west to the Arizona sunshine. The Presbyterian Church had a mission church in Mesa that needed a pastor. When this was to take place, no one knew. As it turned out, a year passed before they made the move west.

It had been a good summer growing together as a family. I had learned a lot about a close-knit family, who unselfishly shared heart and home with all of us. All were treated the same and all cared for each other. It was family fun when Roger's brother Irving, his wife, Phyllis, and their daughters, Caroline and Judy, came for a day. Once in a while, Roger's brother Stanley and his wife, Florence, and children Jim, Alan, Betsy, Barbara, and David came by. Family fun was always exciting. The children hated saying goodbye on these special days. The food, fellowship, and fun were outstanding. We all felt bad that Grace's health caused her to miss it all.

When summer was over, Roger, and I were ready to move back to college. Earl drove us back to Baltimore for a quick visit with my family, who were happy to have us home before we headed off for South Carolina. Brian and Brent were in the back seat with me and Roger and Earl in the front, baggage tucked away in the trunk.

CHAPTER 8

Columbia Bible College

Put on the full armor of God, so that you will
be able to stand firm against the schemes of the
devil.

—Ephesians 6:11

Most of our things were shipped to Columbia Bible College. We left in time to look for a room until our army Quonset hut was ready for occupancy. We found a boarding house that we shared with seven other couples. Sixteen of us were using one bathroom, so we were assigned bathroom times. Even so, morning and evening was an exercise in waiting. Roger and I had good practice at sharing a bathroom that summer living with family.

The boarding house was close to campus, and we were anxious to get the Quonset hut apartment finished. We all were eager to move in and get settled into our new homes. About two months passed and word came that we could move in. I was a junior that year and had been asked to be editor of the yearbook. It was an exciting beginning for the school year.

We were able to buy the furniture we needed with money Roger had saved while he was in the service, and once we got moved in, Roger obtained a large paper route. His sister Winnie had sent some things via truck. School had started, and we were all busy.

We had a wonderful time getting acquainted with others in the Quonset hut. We were all eager to get on with college life so we could head out to serve the Lord. Our apartment was sandwiched between Vi and Max Saltzam and Estella and Bob Mays.

Bible college prepared us for all sorts of things. There were many happy events to mature us to be what God wanted us to be.

I can't praise the Lord enough for all that He did for us at CBC. We were so grateful for the GI funds that came each month to pay for Roger's schooling. My folks kept sending money so that I could continue. Roger had his paper route, and that ten dollars per week put food on the table, a necessary commodity we found out. Dad encouraged us to have good meals on the table, and in turn, we wouldn't have to see doctors as often, reducing those bills. Dad sure was right.

CHAPTER 9

Our Family Grew

Whenever a woman is in labor she had pain, because her hour has come; but when she gives birth to the child, she no longer remembers the anguish because of the joy that a child has been born into the world.

—John 16:21

One morning in October 1946, I awoke feeling pretty rotten and getting up was a chore. I had classes to get to. I felt better during the day, yet I was miserable again the next morning. A terrible pain in my side several weeks later made us decide to see a doctor. I found one, a Dr. Jowers, who was very pleasant and thorough. He assured me that my appendix was just fine, but in June, I would have an addition to the family. I don't know who was more surprised, but we were both excited and very happy to know that a baby would be coming into our home. We loved that baby from the very beginning.

I had just gotten started in the yearbook planning. I had been the assistant editor the previous year and knew with morning sickness and classes, something had to go, so I gave up my job as yearbook editor.

Flossy, Margaret, Ruth, Vi, and Max took classes at the college, and all of us hoped to graduate. I found out soon after that Flossy was expecting Ruth, Margaret was expecting Danny, Vi was expecting Jenny, and I was expecting Linda.

In one of my Bible classes, I met a pretty blonde who saw that I was very uncomfortable sitting at my desk. She started chatting before class began. She started telling me her story, saying she didn't feel so good all the time. She was like me, so naive and not sure what was going on. We kept talking until class started. When the professor got started, I kept thinking on what my new friend had said about not feeling well that morning.

When class was over, we walked along together, and I said, "You ought to see a doctor. He can tell you what's wrong." I had not told her what was going on with me but then told her I was pregnant. I had just found out and didn't want it spread everywhere.

She said, "We have to get to the dining room", and we hurried there.

The dining room featured beautiful white columns, and we ate family style in the dining room. I always loved going there when I was a sophomore and junior. I asked why we were going to the dining room. "My husband George is there, and I want to tell him I could be pregnant," she said.

George was painting the columns, and when we entered, she called up to George, who was working on a ladder. "George," she called up, "I could be pregnant!"

He fell from his perch on the ladder, and we ran to see if he was all right. "Okay," he said. "Oh honey, could I be going to be a dad?"

George grew up an orphan, and they had wanted a baby so badly. He was so excited. They went to see Dr. Jowers that afternoon. That evening they came by our place to tell us that Margaret indeed was going to have a baby. We were all excited. She was due in August 1947, and I was due June that year.

Those nine months were interesting for all of us. We looked forward with joy when our babies would arrive. We were all busy with classes, studying, and taking care of our homes. All of us girls were going to school, so we decided we could take turns babysitting when the time came so each of us would be able to continue classes.

As time got closer in June, it was more exciting. Margaret and George lived off campus. Margaret and Newell, due in September, and Roger and I lived on campus. June came and went for me, but no baby. My mother assured me that I was okay, and as with her, the babies were ten-month babies, and all were big babies. So I rested.

Margaret and George had gone home to York, Pennsylvania, for June and July and were coming back to Columbia in August to have their baby. However, there were slight changes to those plans.

I had been having labor pains, and on July 23, we went to the hospital. I spent the day there, but nothing happened. On Thursday, Friday, and Saturday I felt awful, but Sunday morning, Roger took me back. Dr. Jowers was there and said, "You'll be happy this morning, Meg. Your friend Margaret has had little girl this morning, and she's in the room where you will be after your baby is born."

Many hours later, I delivered a wonderful baby girl and was wheeled into my room. Margaret was all smiles as we chatted about our babies. Nurses brought them both to us, but I was so tired and wanted to sleep. Dr. Jowers wanted me awake for some time until he knew I was all right. I didn't know until later how serious the previous five days had been before Linda was born. I praise the Lord for a friend who was there for me that day and night.

Margaret and George were so happy to have Joyce Faye, born July 27, 1947, and Roger, and I were thrilled to have Linda Louise, born July 27, 1947.

Sadly, Joyce Faye was killed not long after she was married. Margaret and George served in Kenya, Africa, as missionaries with African Inland Mission and then served the Lord in Texas with Wycliffe. Margaret and Newell both worked at Columbia Bible College until the Lord called them home. Their son Danny was born in September after the girls were born. Those times brought so many wonderful memories.

When Roger and I married, I knew little to nothing about cooking. During my year at Wheaton, I started having a skin problem with my hands. I had been to dermatologists and all sorts of other doctors. My dad had spent a small fortune on my hands to no avail. I had been to one doctor in the Chicago area who asked if I was a riveter. I said I wasn't, and he added, "That's what your hands looked like—riveter hands."

Night after night, I just wrapped my hands with coal tar and wore white gloves, but during the day at CBC, I just kept my hands wrapped in gauze. It was an awful time in my life. Yet when I was pregnant, the skin healed and cleared up. But as soon as our babies arrived, back came the bloody cracks in my hands.

I recall ironing Roger's white shirts. I noticed blood on the shirts and had to wash them again. Roger ended up doing the ironing, washing, dishes, baby care, and studying. He never complained, but I felt like a terrible wife and mother. Yet he would encourage me, pray for me, move me, and I praise the Lord for those days of trials.

But what about the mission field with my bloody hands and all? The Lord kept leading each step of the way. My hands were a heavy burden on my heart. Many years later, the Lord saw fit to heal them. Hormones have a strange effect on the body.

Linda was about eighteen months old when I noticed a lump the size of a pea on her left leg. We immediately took her to see Dr. Jowers. He took a careful look and said, "I'll see you at the hospital at 8:00 a.m. tomorrow." It was something to be careful about. We were a bit frightened but prayed that the Lord would be honored in all that had to be done.

When the nurses took Linda into surgery, one said it would be about an hour. One hour turned into several hours, and we were concerned parents. When Dr. Jowers came out, he apologized that it had taken so long. Linda was talking and had to go potty, and they took her, then drink, then potty, and so it went. He said the nurses loved playing with her. So it took longer. The lump turned out to be the size of a walnut. The doctor removed it and was happy with the results.

We had other experiences with Linda.

One morning, I awoke and went to get a crying little girl. We were both exhausted from a sleepless night, and Roger had to get to class. When I touched Linda, she was so hot. I struggled through changing her ammonia diaper.

"Mommy, I'm sick," she cried.

She didn't want to eat, just cry and cry in my arms. I had to wait for Roger to get home so we could take her to the doctor. What had seemed like ages was a relief to have him come home. After looking her over, Dr. Jowers said she needed to be hospitalized. However, he knew we didn't have any money for that, so he told us to give her an aspirin and a teaspoon of water every ten minutes until the fever broke.

I had been fretful about going to Japan, and I had a big concern about Linda. If she got sick, would we understand what was wrong? We knew in our hearts that God would see us through, but this was a hard thing to deal with. We learned another lesson in faith. The same God who was caring for her now would care for her in Japan. But we were scared. Could He do it now? We learned, yes, He could and would.

We arrived home from the doctor, and several of the students who had come by for cookies from time to time were standing at our door. They had seen us carry our bundle of joy and wanted to know what was going on with Linda. As we shared she had virus X, a virus that had no name, but needed time. We gave her fluid for twenty-four hours, a spoonful every ten minutes. A number of our friends volunteered to help us take care of Linda, especially at night so Roger and I could get some sleep. They were as excited as we were to see Linda get better the first day and night as she was the second morning. That was the answer to so many prayers.

Could we be more excited to see God answer prayers? I don't think so. We praised the Lord for those dear young men who sacrificed hours with us to see our daughter be all right in those twenty-four hours. Virus X was no fun, but we saw our faith grow as we trusted Him for Linda and her physical needs.

Linda was a wonderful little girl, but she had some behaviors that needed to be corrected. My best friend Margaret and I would walk downtown through town and back home just about every day. We both were expecting our second babies, and the walking was great for us. Several days in a row, Margaret was very cold to me and didn't care to walk. After a number of days of not seeing her, I stopped by her apartment to see what was wrong. She didn't want me to come in, and that too was strange.

Finally, she said, "Meg, you need to take better control of Linda. Sure she's cute and fun, but she has bitten Danny across the bridge of the nose so often that she has drawn blood."

I was aghast at my daughter's antics and apologized profusely and hugged Margaret. I then left to talk to Linda. When I asked if she had ever bitten Danny, I expected her to say no, but she started crying, and I knew she had done it. I leaned down and bit her across the bridge of her nose, and she screamed.

Hand in hand we walked down to Margaret's house, and Linda apologized to Danny and hugged Aunt Margaret. The children were friends again, and there was no more biting. Our walking to town returned us to our routine.

With so many babies around and more coming all the time, Roger and Max, our neighbor next door, came up with the idea to earn some money so we could go home for Christmas—taking baby pictures for a price that our fellow students could use for Christmas cards. The fellows took the photos and developed the film. Vi and I were involved too by drying prints, packaging them, and seeing that they arrived at the right place. We advertised, and the guys were surprised at how many came to have their babies photographed for grandma and grandpa, etc. It was really a fun project, and the babies were so cute. Some really turned out well, and the business grew enough to provide money to take us home for Christmas.

We found out later that the parents were so pleased to be able to see their grandchildren. Max and Vi's Jennifer and our Linda were good models, so when folks came to order photos, they had some idea how they would turn out.

Max and Vi headed to Minnesota, and we had several fellows go with us to Baltimore for Christmas. We did the picture project for several years, and we all enjoyed working on it.

I found out one day that Vi made her own laundry soap, so I asked if she would teach me how to do it. It was not easy to make, but the results were good as we had very white laundry out on the line.

Our washers were not automatic in any way. My washer bounced back and forth and did a pretty good job but didn't hold much wash.

It was while we were doing laundry one day when Roger said, "You know, I think we could make ice cream with our washing machine." He thought about that for a time, then left to do some shopping. When he came back, he asked me to get a cookbook and mix a batch of vanilla ice cream. Our neighbors pitched in. Some donated eggs, some sugar, some vanilla, and the mixing began. Some chopped ice and others took care of the salting. Roger supervised, but it was a community project. It turned out to be the most delicious ice cream any of us had eaten. Then some came with a concoction of toppings, and we had sundaes. That was a fun project, and we loved it. We did it more than once those last years at CBC.

We had a lot of fun while we were at CBC, and we studied hard and learned all we could about how to plant a church in another culture. There was not much written on the subject, but we sure quizzed missionaries who spoke in chapel to learn all that we could from them.

Our apartment was always a place where others came. I had been in college for two years before Roger got there, so I had some friends from those first two years. Sometimes a couple would come, sometimes a few girls or a few guys. There was someone who decided they needed to spy on the comings and goings at our apartment and then report their findings to the high authorities. Our "spy" reported that couples were "making out" in the living room. When we were called in, we were crushed, but we didn't know if it was true, our apartment was off limits until the end of the semester. The couple was dealt with, but I had little respect for the spy. We found out some time later that the couple was cleared of the accusation, and we were given an apology and cleared. There was no more spying after that.

There are lessons to be learned from many situations that come into a person's life. It is not always easy to accept them when they come. That's why it was so important to keep our eyes on Jesus.

CHAPTER 10

Christian Service: Finding a Church

Therefore if any man is in Christ, he is a new creature; old things passed away; behold new things have become.

—2 Corinthians 5:17

Roger's Christian service during the first year was to work at the state prison. The warden was a Christian and happy for Bible college young men to come. It was a good experience, but Roger was reminded not to give an invitation to come forward after the service because the prisoners were shackled to their benches and couldn't come forward even if they wanted. But there were other ways and several of the prisoners did come to Jesus.

Roger and I long felt we had the best teachers at CBC. We had men of God who lived the Christian life before us and were His examples to want to grow in Jesus.

Another year, Roger came home after school one afternoon with a big smile on his face and much excitement in his voice. The married fellows were asked to go church hunting so they would have some experience preaching. That was just what he had been asking from the Lord. Where to look was the next step. We were told there were many pastored churches nearby in Columbia.

Roger grew up in the Methodist Church. He later joined the Presbyterian Church where I belonged and really came to know the

Lord because of the faithful witness of the GI Gospel Hour in the Philippines. We found prayer was the key to all of this.

Roger went out into the highways and byways around Columbia to find a place to minister. For several days after class, he would head out searching but would come back with no results. Other fellows also were searching. Then after searching for many days, Roger came home with a big smile on his face. "Honey. We have a church," he said.

The church had been closed for eighteen years, and it was the second oldest Southern Baptist church in South Carolina. We had such excitement that evening. A Mrs. Furman had talked with Roger. She had prayed and prayed for someone to come and reopen the High Hills Baptist Church. She had asked if he wanted to go see it. They climbed into Roger's Chevy, and off they went.

The story poured out about what happened that afternoon. I was excited, as they were to know we would be able to achieve another of our goals while at Bible college—getting some experience in church work.

The church sat in the middle of a small run-down cemetery. The outside of the church building was covered with moss dripping from the trees that surrounded the church so thick you could not see the building until you got underneath the moss wall.

Mrs. Furman took out a key from her bag, a skeleton key that Roger said was at least six or seven inches long. She took him to a side door of the dark green-pillared church and was so excited as she opened it. The side door had been the way slaves had entered the church balcony in its early years. He noticed there were no pews upstairs. The slaves had to sit on their feet, and when the offering basket was passed around down below, they had to toss coins into the basket. "They rarely missed a shot," she said. Many of these dear folks really loved the Lord and hated to miss church.

Inside, spiders had taken over decorating without interference. Dust was thick on the rustic pews downstairs, altar furniture, communion table, as well as on the hymnbooks in the pews and on the pump organ.

Mrs. Furman said we could come Sunday and start meetings. She had no idea how many people in and around Horatio would come, but she felt some would come and help us clean the first time. We hardly could wait for Sunday to arrive. We had no idea what was going to happen, but we took work and church clothing for the occasion. In the meantime, we heard that some Baptist students found a Presbyterian church to serve in, and the Presbyterian now had a Baptist church. By Sunday, I don't know who was more excited and happy.

Horatio was a whistle-stop on a train line; the train didn't stop unless it was signaled to stop. The town was a few miles off Highway 378 between Columbia and Sumter. It was a cotton growing area of South Carolina. The town had two stores. One housed the post office, had the only filling station, and sold ice cream and candy. The other store was a country store that carried everything someone would need to live on—food, clothes, etc. A large potbelly stove was located in the corner of the large room, and sitting around it were men and women talking and sharing the news of the day.

It was a happy gossip spot, and many came to hear and to share. When we walked in that first time, they all knew Brother Fox had come to open High Hills Baptist Church. We were generously welcomed into the community. That first Sunday was the beginning of three of the happiest years of our lives where we learned to trust the Lord for everything.

As we were making our way into the church, we heard car doors closing, and as we looked behind us, families were winding their way to the open door. Roger had the skeleton key, and when he opened the door that first day, the church was spotless. Mrs. Furman had said she had no idea how many people would come, but she knew there were some who would be loyal to the old church.

I expected someone would play the organ, but when no one did, Roger said, "My wife will play." Smiles stretched across faces as we sang some of their favorites—"The Old Rugged Cross," "Nearer, My God, to Thee," "At Calvary," and "One Day," and on and on. I wasn't the greatest piano player as almost every hymn I had trouble hitting the right notes at the end of each song. I wanted to end each song correctly but almost never made it; however, everyone sang to the end with me in spite of my mistakes.

We made many new friends that day. Mrs. Hattie and Uncle Bob invited us to dinner at their home. Roger always said between Hattie's chicken and his mom's chicken, he would have a hard time saying which was the best. We often stayed with Cleo and Julie and their two children as they had more room than the others in Horatio. We ate meals in a lot of homes, and they became dear families to us. Looking back, I still remember those wonderful days with fondness, as we were there every Sunday, Wednesday, and sometimes Saturdays. Few wanted to miss any of the gatherings. When I think back to those days, I praise the Lord for lessons learned.

One Wednesday night, before prayer meeting, a woman who had often gone to the beauty shop who had grown to know and love the Lord Jesus shared, "I used to go to the beauty shop to gossip and to hear all the dirt there was going on in and around Horatio. Now I go to share about Jesus with the women. Some laugh at me, but now others are coming to church."

When the town drunk accepted Jesus, he was full of joy. He drank milk after his salvation to rid himself of the liquor he had spent so much time drinking. He truly was a new creature in Jesus. The old had passed away, and the new was his delight. He couldn't get enough of the Word in his heart.

The men in the community loved to hunt, and so did Roger, so some Wednesdays, we would head there early in the afternoon so we could let the guys hunt before prayer meeting. We would go Saturdays, and us girls would have some gab sessions while the men would hunt squirrels in the "Santa Swamps."

One Saturday, one of the men, James, had gotten a new Bluetick Coonhound, a breed that was known for being good for hunting squirrels. Before the men had been gone for not even an hour, the dog was back under the house. The men kept hunting and then came home for a big catfish and hot biscuit dinner. When they returned, we asked them what had happened with the dog. They said someone fired at a squirrel, and the dog ran. Turned out the "hunting" dog was gun-shy. The pup was returned and traded for a new hound that really did love squirrel hunting.

Roger found that the people were really hungry for God's Word. He preached on Christian living, lessons from Joshua, and the truth about the beginning of the world. For weeks, he preached on the power of God, who Jesus is, and why go overseas with the gospel. Almost every week, someone accepted Jesus as his or her personal Savior. Sunday school classes got off the ground for the children. Some adults, who never had taught before, learned how to be teachers.

Sometimes on Sunday, we would take another person with us to share their testimony. One of the young men at CBC was a fellow from China. We always loved to hear him talk about the need for someone to go to his country to share about Jesus. He'd have dinner in the evening with us. Linda was still young at that time, but she loved to hear him share his story.

He learned from us too about American food. One night, we had hot dogs. We saw how he ate his, like Linda fixed hers, plain with a little bit of oleo. Then he would try one like Roger's with ketchup and mustard. Then it was my turn, and I loved onions on mine. He finally tried all three, and I asked which he liked best. He replied, "Plain like Linda's."

He also enjoyed spaghetti, but his favorite with us was fried chicken and mashed potatoes. We learned a good bit about his homeland. It was always good to have foreign students take part in the church.

It was after we had been working in Horatio maybe a year when Roger, Linda, and I were coming into town for church. We had crossed the train tracks and started past the country store when Roger put on the brakes quickly to stop in front of the store. "Look," he said, pointing at the front window. "Sunday morning, and the store is closed."

A big sign across the front of the window read, "Horatio Country Store is closed from now on, on Sunday, because God's Word says to 'Remember the Sabbath Day and keep it Holy.' Exodus 20:8."

We were so surprised by all the men and women that were in church that morning. A more joyful group you have never seen. All, that is, except for the couple that ran the post office, filling station, and ice cream shop across the street from the country store. They didn't think it was right to close both places. About two weeks later, when we pulled into town, both stores were closed, and the whole town was in church. What joy there was, for Sundays were for the Lord, and all the surrounding community knew why. "God said so."

Roger, Linda, and I were always there for Sunday school and church and Wednesdays for prayer meeting. We never knew which house we were to go to, but we really didn't have any problems finding folks.

Roger had kept up his paper route all through college, delivering about eighty papers each day out in the suburbs of Columbia. I'd drive, and he tossed papers to the porches and yards. One of Roger's professors, Don Hoke, was on our route, and his wife Martha usually had a plate of chocolate chip cookies for us to enjoy. We always enjoyed the drop-in visits and the cookie plate. Their son Don and our Linda both were two years old and had become fast friends.

During Roger's senior year at CBC, he went to do his paper route one particular week, and his boss informed him that he was giving all of the married guys' paper routes to high school kids, and no amount of discussion was going to change his mind.

That ten-dollar job had put food on our table all those years. When I fussed about it, Roger took me in his arms and said, "Honey, we have some lessons to learn about trusting the Lord. He said He will supply all of our needs. I believe He will. I will now have more time to do my homework and to prepare for my church work for Sundays and Bible study on Tuesday nights.

"We have been praying so much for the people in High Hills to come to Jesus, and now, without our job, we can go to the Billy Graham Crusade training sessions and learn how to help people who come to the prayer room. We've been asking the Lord to do this, and now, we can go and be counselors for the crusade that is coming to Columbia."

We hugged and prayed together and praised the Lord. We decided not to tell anyone at the church that we lost our food money, and we would see how the Lord would take care of us. We prayed and asked the Lord to supply our food money just as He had cared for us up to that point.

This was a really special time to see God work. We both knew God was calling us to work in Japan as missionaries. I was beginning to grow large with baby number two and was wondering where the money was going to come from, but Roger always said, "The Lord knows our needs." He did too. Our trust was in Him for all that we had to face. He never failed us.

The loss of the paper route was on a Monday. Wednesday, we were to drive the forty miles to Horatio. We always liked going early so we could visit with the church folks. We seemed to have an open door and the folks had troubles that needed prayer. Roger was excellent with sharing God's Word with troubled hearts. It was wonderful to be wanted.

We pulled into a yard behind a school bus. Boys and girls were tumbling out of the bus. We heard one of the boys say to his buddy, "Remember to come to prayer meeting tonight. We're going to pound the preacher."

Roger and I looked at each other and said, "What's a pounding?"

We heard it again at another house: "We're going to pound the preacher."

We decided to go to Cleo's. Neither of us said anything to her. We had a good supper, and it wasn't long before it was time for prayer meeting. People started coming in, and they all seemed so happy to see us. What could a pounding be?

The living room was full at the normal starting time. They shared requests and prayed through the list. Singing praise songs, and Roger's message on faith seemed to hit the spot, and it was over.

Cleo said, "Don't anyone leave. We have something to share," and the ladies disappeared. Next thing we knew, the ladies came back with bundles of packages and laid them at our feet. We looked in astonishment as we began to unwrap as we were told to do.

Cleo would stop us from opening certain packages. We found out why. Some of the packages were frozen, and she didn't want the freezer paper torn. A pound of butter, a pound of bread, a pound of cheese, a pound of beans—we were being pounded—and the list kept growing. It was a pile of food like we had never seen before. "You lost your food money," we heard God say, "but I'm taking care of you."

With tears in our eyes, Roger shared with the folks what had happened Monday with Roger losing the paper route. They asked why we didn't tell them, and Roger told them we thought God would supply all of our needs without telling anyone. This was the beginning of His supply for needs that I'll share as this story unfolds. That may have been the first time I thought of the words I carried close to my heart for the rest of my life—Jesus Never Fails.

Our trip home that evening was full of praise and joy. We had always purchased one chicken each week. Roger would cut it into ten pieces, and we each had a piece for each evening during the week. When Linda became old enough, one chicken didn't last the week. A pound of pork, a pound of roast—it was wonderful. Everyone was so happy. That was our first pounding, but it wasn't our last one. It seemed that when the food supply was about gone, the Lord provided. One of the families at the church even filled our gas tank each week. That answered another prayer about how we were going to pay for that.

We were thrilled to share how God provided for us. We enjoyed the counseling sessions when it got near to the Billy Graham Crusade coming. We talked up the meetings to the church folks but knew it would be hard for the cotton farmers to attend. Some folks did faithfully pray for us and the meetings.

Much to our surprise, while we were in the counseling room at the end of the meetings, many came forward and came back to the prayer room. What a sight to behold as one by one over the week of meetings, our dear folks from High Hills, farmers and all, met us in the prayer room and accepted Jesus as their personal Savior. Seventeen of our church members accepted Christ that week in church and at the Billy Graham Crusade. Our hearts were so full when we got back to our apartment. We couldn't stop talking and praising the Lord. Those who were not making salvation decisions were rededicating their lives to Jesus.

The following week, we had a new family at High Hills. Testimonies flowed. Communities around heard what had taken place. It was a thrilling time in the life of the church.

Then there were some trials that stretched our faith. We were planning on going to prayer meeting one week when Roger came home with a glum look on his face. When I asked him what was wrong, he told me the car had broken down and was in the garage. Mahar had helped him get it into a garage. Something was broken. What are we going to do?

"We are going to pray," Roger said. "We need eighty-three dollars to pay for it, and it will be ready Wednesday."

He then asked me how much money we had, and I told him we had five dollars in birthday money last year from the folks. Now, in those days, eighty-three dollars was a large sum of money. We just didn't have that kind of money sitting in our account. So we went to prayer, and as we got up from our knees, Roger saw Maxwell walk by and called out, "Could you lend me eighty-three dollars for Wednesday until I can get it or until the Lord provides."

He said sure, and Roger sighed in relief.

That was another big first in living by faith. We had some lessons to learn. Roger came home from college with the mail. He opened some letters and handed each to me. My roommate Ann had come from Michigan, and a friend of hers had purchased something from us but didn't have the money to pay us at the time. Inside one of the envelopes was a check for eighty-nine dollars to cover that purchase. Roger took that check to the garage to pick up the car.

The mechanic said, "Mr. Fox, I made an error on your bill. It is eighty-nine dollars."

We learned that day that the Lord could and would care for us in our time of need. It was not our first lesson in faith, and it certainly was not our last.

The church people grew in their faith and love of Jesus too. Those three years of working at High Hills Baptist Church gave us a lot of experience to prepare for the work of church planting that we would do in Japan in the years ahead.

CHAPTER 11

Answering God's Call

How then will they call on Him in whom they
have not believed? And how will they hear without
a preacher. How will they preach unless they are
sent? Just as it is written, How beautiful are the
feet of those who bring good news of good things.

—Romans 10:14–15

Roger's graduation class at CBC was a terrific group. Most of
those fellows had served in World War II, and all branches of
the military were represented. All were eager to graduate and
go forth to serve the Lord. Each checked out mission boards, and just
about all were going out as church planters. The whole senior year,
each senior felt God's call to go forth with one thing in mind—we
must learn all we can to be the best prepared in the areas to which
we were going. Eighty-five were going to the mission field from the
class, which was pretty awesome. Each had chosen a mission field
and knew where they were going. There were none with "wishy-
washy" answers when asked if and when they were going. It was a
very exciting time of their lives.

We had been praying for the right mission board to open the
door that we were to go with when a medium-sized brown envelope
arrived. Roger tore it open, and there was a brochure in sepia with
the words "500 missionaries to 5 million Japanese in five years." We

read it from cover to cover, and we both felt this was the mission board for us. It was from the Far Eastern Gospel Crusade (FEGC) in Minneapolis, Minnesota, with General Director Philip Armstrong, who also had served during the war in Japan.

We were impressed and gave us such a desire to go with this board that over and over, we knew this was God's place for us. Roger wrote a letter and shared his heart and desire to meet with the board. A letter came back that said there would be a meeting in August at Winona Lake in Indiana. Four years of training was coming to a close. We were stepping out by faith to see God take us to Japan in the very near future.

I was excited about a new bundle of joy in my tummy. Our Timothy was on the way and due the middle of June 1950, and graduation was the month before. We figured Tim would be born in June, and then after graduation, we would have July to clean up our apartment before heading to Winona Lake in August to be part of the FEGC conference. But God had other plans.

Tim was a 10-month baby, like his sister, and was born July 13. He was such a beautiful and happy baby, and we were blessed. When Roger and Linda came to pick up Tim and me at the hospital, the nurse who was carrying Tim held him down for Linda to see and uncovered him. "Look, Dad, he has a head and feet too," she exclaimed.

I'm not sure what she had expected, but we all had a good laugh as she hugged her baby brother. What joy and happiness there was in our home. But as was the case in those days, my doctor put stipulations on my activities for the next six to eight weeks. That made moving a chore and leaving school was not easy. It took more time than we expected.

The apartment was empty, the car was packed, and the four of us were ready to leave. Roger had made a wonderful oversized drawer with a harness that fit into the back seat of our car so that Tim could sleep in it, and as he grew, could sit up and play in it. He spent a lot of time in that drawer in those days, and both of our kids were secure as we traveled. We arrived at Winona Lake and found a large number of young couples like ourselves who were excited as much as we were about the brochure they too had received.

We stepped up to the desk, and Roger asked for a first floor-room for the four of us, if that was possible. A young man who, looked at our application papers, looked at us with a funny look but reluctantly assigned us a first-floor room overlooking the lake. We hustled to unpack and get the children settled and took a little nap. It had been a long trip from Columbia to Baltimore to leave some of our baggage, then on to Winona Lake. That was the first of many trips on our way to the mission field. We wondered what would be next in our travels, but we knew we were not alone. The Lord would be with us.

There were so many people at conference, and the people on the board were happy to see all of us there. The meetings we attended had special music that was wonderful. The Bible messages were rich in blessing. It was exciting to hear the needs of Japan, Okinawa, and the Philippines that were laid out for us to know what we would be facing.

There were a few challenges to face as we were assigned a time to meet the mission board. Someone was assigned to babysit the children as the adults met with the board during special evening hours. Our time came, and with some trepidation, we went into this large room, where there was a large circle of men. It was pretty intimidating, but Roger had said we had nothing to fear. We are ready to go to Japan to serve the Lord to plant churches, that the Lord had brought us that far and would see us all the way. He squeezed my hand three times, which was his usual way of saying "I love you," and I quieted down after that.

The very first question they asked was by an unmarried board member, who wondered why I couldn't take a room on the second or third floor. Roger hadn't bothered to give a reason when he asked for a first-floor room during registration. He just figured that everyone would know after they saw me with a tiny newborn, but it didn't register. So I told him my baby was two weeks old, and I had doctor orders not to climb stairs or lift heavy objects for six weeks. That was the normal procedure those days after giving birth. I'm afraid I made him blush, and he apologized for his attitude earlier that day in assigning us a room.

Then the board asked, "Roger, you and Meg are Presbyterian Church members. We wonder where you stand on infant baptism."

Roger just said he had never given much thought about it.

Then he was asked, "Do you believe in a believer's baptism?" and we didn't know how to answer. We didn't know the right answers and wondered where this was going.

Things quieted down, and we were asked to come back. As we walked out, we were a bit confused. R. E. Thompson, a wonderful man with an Irish brogue, caught up with us and said he was sorry for the discussions in the boardroom. He came to our room and explained what they were looking for. We did believe in believer's baptism, and we knew baby baptism was not right.

R. E. gave us some material to read and "see if this fits your beliefs." We really were green by all the questions about where we stood on baptism. We read and looked up the verses; we realized we hadn't given the answers the board members had wanted.

R. E. was such a great mentor. He and his wife Ella had spent thirty years as missionaries with China Inland Mission before the Japanese army overran the school where they had been working. After the war, they continued their work until the communist Chinese government put an end to missionary work.

Because of their experience, R. E. was asked to help outgoing missionaries prepare for the field. He spent a good amount of time with us so that by the time we were called back to meet the board, we knew what we believed and why, and when they asked questions, our answers came from our hearts.

There was no question that we would fit in with the mission. We had a good evening, and our single gentleman friend was sorry he had not thought through the questions or that he had not come directly to us to see why I couldn't climb stairs.

We were accepted as a group one evening before we left Winona Lake. We were members of the Far Eastern Gospel Crusade and assigned to Japan as church planters. We learned a great deal during that conference that week. We knew the Lord had placed us in this mission and that He had a job for us to do.

We learned about the need of the Japanese for Christ, the living conditions of a foreign country, that we most likely would be isolated from other missionaries, and what we could look forward to learning the language and about the culture.

All of us were in hopes of getting to the field the following year, 1951. We all had many questions, and we kept R. E. Thompson and Phil Armstrong really busy answering them. There was no question not worthy of an answer, and those two did their very best to answer all of them.

New friends also were made that week—Rollie and Esther Reasoner, Johnny and Anna Seibert, Rollie and Jean Friesen, Jack and Grace Frizen, Sydney and Dorothy Best, Dick and Claudia Blevins, Bob and Dorothy Matheson, Shelton and Arlene Allen, Bertha Neufeld, Marie Olfert, Dorothy Jeanes, Winnie Price, Doris Hume, Wanda Lautzenheiser, and Conrad Miller.

We all knew that God had a wonderful plan for our lives. We were to see the steps unfold just as the children of Israel went through the Jordan River. By faith, we put our feet forward.

CHAPTER 12

Getting Ready to Go

Be anxious for nothing, but in everything by prayer and supplication with thanksgiving let your requests be made known to God. And the peace of God, which surpasses all comprehension, shall guard your hearts and your minds in Christ Jesus.

—Philippians 4:6–7

Preparations for going to Japan kept falling into place. We arrived back in Baltimore after a wonderful week at Winona Lake conference grounds, where we became a part of Far Eastern Gospel Crusade. Phil Armstrong, the director, made each of us feel very much a part of the mission.

We were excited about going to Japan to take God's Word to the people who had been our enemy during World War II. However, we wanted to take the gospel to these dear people. We had now enlisted, so to speak, in ministry with FEGC. We did not know what it all meant, but we had assurance He was leading and we were willing to follow.

Roger's mom was okay with our going because his folks already had spent three years living with the thoughts that their baby boy was going overseas during the war and most likely would not be coming back. They were joyfully surprised when he did return home. Now he was going again for God, and she was cheerful about it all, loved us, and loved our little girl and little boy. Papa Fox passed away not too many months after Linda was born in 1947.

Mama had always been happy when we went to see her in Totowa. She had many good friends there, and a door was opened to share, and out of that church group, the Lord gave us some faithful prayer warriors. Roger and I were convinced from the very beginning that prayer was the key to our getting all that was needed to make it possible for us to go.

September was off to a good start. The four of us moved in with my parents. My sister Alice was off at Wheaton College. My brother Marvin was there too from time to time but that winter was away at Fuller Theological Seminary in California. He had moved out when we moved in so there was plenty of room. Mom was so happy to have the children. She loved both of them, her first grandchildren.

Roger was laying out plans as to how to get it across to people that we were going to Japan. We began to share the news simply so as to not look like we were begging. We both were positive that if the Lord wanted us in Japan, He simply would provide all we needed without folks knowing we needed money to go.

That first Sunday, a dear elderly friend of my parents greeted us in church with, "Do you know how much money you will need to go to Japan?"

She was a widow who lived with her daughter. She wanted to pledge ten dollars a month for our needs. Before we had said anything to anyone, she came forth. Her monthly pledge came every month until the Lord called her home several years later. Her daughter picked up that pledge and continued to support us. How I praise the Lord Jesus for her faithfulness to Him. That was the beginning of the Lord moving us on. We watched Him provide all that we needed.

Doors opened for us to share what we were going to do. Dad had good contacts in Baltimore through the Presbyterian Church. Then because it was slow coming, he had a board meeting in New York City with Presbyterians. He was gone for a weekend, and when he came home, he was really excited. At the dinner table, he shared this weekend in New York. He had gone to the Presbyterian Mission

Board headquarters to see if we couldn't go with them and all our financial needs would be met.

"Really nice idea, Dad," Roger said. "What became of the visit?"

"If you were from Maryville or Princeton instead of Wheaton and Columbia Bible College, you'd fit in fine in Japan, but Korea is different, and you'd be wanted, and all of your financial needs would be cared for," Dad said. "There are lots of people to reach in Korea."

"Dad, we're grateful for your loving care and concern, but we feel like the Lord is taking us to Japan."

"I know, Roger," Dad continued. "I will back you in prayer and encouragement and financially as I can as you go with FEGC."

My Presbyterian dad, who really loved Jesus, was happy we were going with FEGC, a faith mission board. He prayed for us, encouraged us, and gave as the Lord allowed him and was a rich blessing. He and Mother were supportive. It was wonderful knowing that my parents were on board with us going overseas.

Those days in September through January 1950–51 were busy for all of us. Mother was wonderful with the children. She loved playing with them and taking them for walks. When the children were happy, it was good for all of us.

Lots of letters went out. Doors opened to speak in churches in Ocean City, New Jersey, and all around Baltimore. In one of those churches, it was decided that Roger should be ordained. It was a lovely service, and all who came were so excited to see Roger ordained. He still was attached to the army air corps reserves, so the next step was to clear him from military service. Mail began to come from people that we didn't know, but they knew we were going overseas. Church doors were open, and people wanted to do something to help us take the gospel to the Japanese. Step-by-step, we saw that God was leading.

In October, we had some orientation classes to go to in Minnesota. When we arrived, we were assigned to the home of Shirley and Monna Reasoner. We had met their son Rollie and his wife Esther when we were at the Winona Lake conference. They were a wonderful couple and made us feel so much at home.

We learned a great deal that week with our mentor R. E. Thompson in charge. He was born and raised in Belfast, Ireland, in 1897 and accepted Christ at a young age and had a burden to go tell the Chinese about Jesus. We loved listening to his Irish brogue and his wisdom as to how to get a church started was fascinating. He was a long-winded speaker, and Roger set some alarm clocks over the room so they would go off every few minutes because he wasn't the only teacher we had. Things had to keep moving. It didn't take long for R. E. to learn that when a clock alarm sounded, he had to let us go.

It was wonderful getting to know Phil Armstrong. He was always strikingly dressed and shared with all of us ragtag missionaries coming out of Bible college. We did not have the money to spend for clothes and other materials to attend all dressed up.

Phil explained to us that we were to be a testimony in our appearance and our message as we pulled up to a new church. Have diapers washed and clean, except for what the baby was wearing. Disposable diapers did not exist then. We didn't need fancy things; just be clean and look nice. Slacks were unheard of for ladies, so we had to get some things for our times of ministry. Phil used to say we should dress as unto the Lord. "You are His witnesses. Let others see Jesus in you."

It was amazing how so many things fell into place. The Bible messages in the Old Testament were refreshing, and as God took care of the people in those days, He was willing to take care of us too.

Galatians 2:20 was very real. "I have been crucified with Christ; and it is no longer I who live, but Christ lives in me; and the life which I now live in the flesh I live by faith in the Son of God, who loved me, and gave Himself up for me."

Our trip back to Baltimore was a long ride, but it gave us time to reflect on what we had learned in Minnesota. The folks were happy to see us come home. Linda and Tim were happy to see us also, though they had enjoyed their time with Grandma and Grandpa. We had contentment knowing that the children were happy to be with my folks. Trips to Totowa were important to see Mama Fox, aunts and uncles, nieces and nephews, and longtime friends.

By faith, we were moving on little by little and support came in. We needed 325 dollars a month support plus outgoing expenses. We were asked to come to Ocean City Baptist Church in New Jersey for a Wednesday night prayer meeting and after we spoke, the janitor and his wife invited us to stay overnight with them. We were taken to their four-story shore home. She was a collector of all sorts of things, so it was like a curio shop, and we loved seeing all their goodies.

Refreshments were served, and we started talking about Japan as to why we wanted to go there and what we had hoped of doing. They asked if we had done some reading, and Roger said, "Yes, we had five books to read, which were rare but were in English."

It was 3:30 in the morning when we finally stopped and went to bed for some much-needed sleep. Bed felt good, but morning came early. Ruthie, their four year old, woke early, so the rest of us did, too. Al and Ruth had some questions, and when we finished our time together, we pulled away from Ocean City just before noon with a promise of support that changed and increased over time. The church was very mission-minded and involved. They wrote that they would keep in touch because they wanted to share in our support. Al and Ruth wanted their Sunday school class to take some of our support too.

Forest Park Presbyterian Church also supported us. The people were very happy that we were going to Japan to share Jesus with our World War II enemy. North Avenue Presbyterian Church joined in too to help us with our support needs. It was always an excitement when the men from the church would come and ask how the church could help us. The Lord knew our heart's desire, for we didn't mention our needs unless someone asked. It was a wonderful few months in preparation to go.

One day, we received a list in the mail of the things we needed to take the Japan. Heading the list was two pairs of women's wool slacks. When Mother read the list, she was not happy that I needed "men's clothing" to go to the mission field. But we felt there had to be a good reason. I bought two pairs of slacks and tucked them away for later use.

It seemed all was going so well, but then the money stopped coming in. It compelled us to pray. "Lord, Jesus, do you really want us to go to Japan?"

Roger prayed. "Could you please send us a token gift of five dollars so we will know the rest is coming?"

The next morning, a letter arrived from Florida from a woman we did not know with a promise of five dollars a month support. We knew the rest would come in, and it did.

We spoke nearly every Sunday, Roger in the pulpit and me in Sunday school. One Sunday, I was to speak to a class, and Roger was speaking to the adults. Just as I stood up, a little boy in this class stood to his feet and said, "You're not a fox, and you don't have a bushy tail," and sat down so disappointed. The teacher had primed the class that there were some foxes coming to share in Sunday school and church and were heading to Japan to tell the Japanese about Jesus. The boy had expected a real fox to be speaking that day. When the class was over, he came up to tell me that he was happy I was going to Japan.

One evening at home, our doorbell rang, and there was my dad's associate in the Pocket Testament League. He asked if he could have some help. Roger went with him to his car and took out a strange-looking box. When they got it into the house, they opened it and pulled out a small but wonderful portable organ, pump style. I was so surprised. He said it was from the Pocket Testament League for me to have to make music when our first church was started.

That little organ went to Japan with us and was used in tent meetings and home services for many years and was such a source of blessing to the family. That organ was the icing on the cake for things to take to Japan.

CHAPTER 13

Hard to Say Goodbye

For I am convinced that neither death, nor life, nor angels nor principalities, nor things present, nor things to come, nor powers, nor height, nor depth, nor any other created thing, will be able to separate us from the love of God, which is in Christ Jesus our Lord.

—Romans 8:38–39

Convinced? Yes! God had called us to Japan to share the good news of the gospel to the people with whom we had been at war.

Christmas was a wonderful time for us as 1950 was closing. We knew that 1951 held some challenges for us that only the Lord could see us through. We said our goodbyes and hugged and hugged Mom and Dad. As Dad prayed for us, we knew we were doing what God wanted. It was not easy. In fact, it was really difficult.

The car was packed with all of our belongings. The large drawer Roger had made for Tim was wonderful for his safety in our travels. He could sleep in it as well as sit up in it and play with his toys. Linda had her books, her toys, and her doll and was excited to get going on our first trip across the United States.

Just as we were about the pull away from the curb, Dad asked Roger if he had money with which to travel. Roger said he had fifty dollars and that the Lord promised to take care of all our needs. We pulled away after thanking them so much for their loving care of us. Just about all of our needs had been met. Mother had prepared wonderful sandwiches for us as she usually did for our trips, so it was just easy stop and go then move on.

We arrived in Columbia, South Carolina, that first day. Margaret and Newell were ready for us. Danny and Joel were young like Linda and Tim. Visiting with friends at CBC always was good. We had so much for which to be thankful. Newell worked at CBC before and after graduation. He also played the organ at church, and it was a joy to hear him play. Our friendship lasted until the Lord called them home

Before we knew it, it was time to head south to our first speaking engagement at a church in St. Petersburg, Florida. What a welcome we had upon arrival. The pastor was warm and friendly. The treasurer took us to a lovely small motel to freshen up and be ready to speak that evening. He visited with us and told us how to get to the church. Someone was coming to take us to supper beforehand. It was a large Methodist Church, and the place was buzzing with activity. There were so many people at this evening service and was wonderful.

The pastor introduced Roger as a young man who accepted Christ while in the Philippines as a fighter pilot while serving in the army air corps, and now his family was heading back to Japan to take the good news to the Japanese. He then told Roger the pulpit was his before sitting down.

The kindness of the pastor and the warmth of the congregation overwhelmed Roger. Roger told me later he never felt such joy as he opened his Bible to speak. He spoke about the blind man whom Jesus made to see and how he had prayed that many blind in Japan would come to know the Lord in their hearts.

After Roger finished, the pastor stood and told the congregation he had no idea if the Foxes had any needs, but he imagined that they did. He said, "Mr. Fox has eight pockets in his suit and all are empty. Instead of taking an offering, I want you to come forward and fill his pockets and wish the Foxes well as they go across the United

States and the Pacific Ocean to the Japanese who not long ago were our enemy."

People from all over came and shook our hands, hugged us, and cried. They wanted to know how long it would take to sail across the Pacific. One lady handed me a picture of her husband and asked when I saw him to tell him that she was fine. There was no address, just a quick glimpse at the picture, and she tucked it back into her purse.

An older gentleman shook Roger's hand and tucked something hard into it and said, "Mail it back before you leave the country." Roger handed it to me and went on talking with those who came by.

The song leader closed the service with "Blest Be the Ties That Bind" and then a prayer. The treasurer said he would meet us at the motel so that we could count the money together. We were so grateful for a pastor with a heart and compassion for the Lord's work. He thanked us for coming, and we thanked him for allowing us to be there. It was an evening that we never forgot and treasured so many times.

The treasurer was right behind us as we entered the motel room. He asked if we had any idea how much money might be in Roger's pockets, but we had no idea. All Roger had done was shake people's hands, and the people stuffed his pockets. Money came from every area of his suit. Roger said it was a strange feeling to have this happen.

As the money was counted and the total disclosed, we were floored. We told the treasurer about my dad's question, "Did we have enough to go across the country?" and Roger's telling him we had fifty dollars. That fifty dollars was well used up by the time we reached Florida. I handed Roger the card that he had given me and he asked the treasurer about it.

"Don't you know what this is?" he asked. It was a Gulf Oil credit card. We could go to a Gulf gas station, pump the gas, pay for the gas with the card, and then continue using it all the way across the country. We had never seen one. We were surprised and grateful.

After a hearty breakfast, we headed to our next destination. That envelope of money took care of our needs to the very penny for the rest of our trip. God's work—it was He who provided it for us.

That Florida church also took care of fifty dollars per month in support and continued for the full five years until we returned home on furlough in 1956. We had a letter from them that their project was finished and thanked us for our endeavors in Japan. We sent quarterly letters to them, but we never did hear from them again.

Along the way, we shared books about Japan. I read most of the time on the road or we counted animals along the highway. It was not easy going to Japan. The closer the time came for us to leave, it became more apparent what we were going to be facing.

Fish heads and rice seemed to be the general opinion of what we would be eating. We had shipped three fifty-five-gallon drums full of pots and pans, clothing for five years, as well as bedding. It was meager wares to keep up housekeeping. We didn't have much in the way of "things," so we would be content with what we had. We had gotten rid of most everything in Columbia and Horatio. So we shipped those three drums along with my college steamer trunk. All were painted blue with an orange stripe so they would be easy to find at Japanese customs. We learned later this proved to be an excellent idea.

Our next stop was in Mesa, Arizona. January in Arizona was wonderful—warm days, cool nights. Earl had moved his family to Mesa in 1947 when they found out that Grace had tuberculosis and had little time to live, or so they thought. Her first doctor said he would like to use her as a guinea pig and see if he could extend her life. In 1948, she had surgery on her lungs. She had come through her surgery and was slowing gaining back her strength. She lived to tell the story for many, many years later. Mama Fox was so happy to see us and greeted us with open arms. She had been staying with Earl and Grace.

Earl and Grace's sons Brian and Brent loved Linda and Tim. The boys had a horse corralled at the church that they took care of and rode. It was a great time for the kids.

Roger said he would like to retire in Mesa one day. The weather was wonderful. Little did we know that we would live there someday but not as retirees. Our time in Mesa was more than we could ever have imagined. We met some wonderful people. Earl opened doors where we could share, and we had choice time with Mama.

After a few days with them, we had to move on. Goodbyes never are easy and those were especially tough. Mama Fox waved us out of sight. We knew she was not well. Her kidneys had been giving her trouble for a long time. Roger was very quiet but drove on to California. Mama Fox died July 13 that summer of 1951 after we had arrived in Japan.

My brother lived in Pasadena, California, while he was attending Fuller Theological Seminary. We stopped for a visit with him. He was happy to see us and had made some wonderful arrangements for us to stay in the home of new friends who welcomed us royally and made us feel so much at home. California was everything we had heard it to be. Skies were so blue, and flowers were blooming everywhere along the side of the road.

We spoke in our new friend's church on Sunday and added more names to our mailing list. There were so many people to write to share the work the Lord called us to do. Another lady wanted to know how long it was going to take to drive to Japan. I don't know why those people weren't in geography class that day, but in those days, a ship was the preferred method of travel across the ocean. All too soon, it was more goodbyes as we had to leave the Los Angeles area and headed to San Francisco. It seemed like a long trip, but Linda and Tim were happy, and that made it an easier journey.

* * * * *

The Home of Peace in San Francisco was a haven for China missionaries for many years. Missionaries needed a place to go out from and which to return. It was a huge home with many halls to many bedrooms. We received a warm welcome from the other missionaries heading for Japan.

The Bests, Blevins, Reasoners, Sieberts, Conrad Miller, Bertha Neufield, and children, mostly babies and young school-age children were at the home. The Blevins had school-age Jenny Sue, and the Bests had three boys. Sarah Reasoner, the same age as Tim, and Leroy and Cherry Siebert all had the measles when we arrived at the Peace Home.

The freighter workers from the ship on which we were to sail were on strike. We knew that when the strike was over, we could sail, but then we received word that if anyone had measles, leaving was out of the question. So we settled in for a long spring. Linda and Tim needed to get shots for measles and even then, we didn't know if they would have them or not. So we waited. Prayer was all-important to us.

Money was dwindling as we paid our bills to stay there. We planned on selling our Chevy before we left, but our delay meant that the sale would have to be done at the right time, or we would be without a way to get around.

After several weeks, Hugh and Dorothy Brown and son Danny arrived. They had so many stories to tell. Dorothy said Hugh had never driven a car until that trip, so they took all the side roads to avoid driving on fast highways. We all could see him creeping along on back roads. It took them a lot longer that way. And on top of that, Danny had diarrhea and was a sick little boy.

Finally, we received word that the freighters were going to sail in two weeks. Then time flew. Marvin came to San Francisco to see us off, and after a week or so, had to get back to the seminary in Los Angeles. It was really hard for me to say goodbye to my brother. We had such a great visit. He was talking about going to the mission field and had a girl to talk things over with but nothing had been decided.

One morning, after Marvin left, we were walking in the cool air, and the phone rang. Someone called out, "It's for the Foxes!"

Who could be calling us? Roger, Linda, and I each got a phone. Then we heard Dad's voice from his office, Mother from home, my sister Alice at Wheaton College, and Marvin from Fuller Seminary after Dad had called roll call. What a reunion we had. It was so special.

Dad read some verses and prayed for us all, and Mother closed by singing,

Turn your eyes upon Jesus.
Look full in His wonderful face.

And the things of Earth will grow strangely dim.
In the light of His glory and grace.

I don't think there was a dry eye as phones clicked our good-byes. The thought hit we might never see each other again nor hear their voices either. It was a very sobering evening, and there was not much talking as we headed for bed. Roger was so tender that evening. He just sat and held me in his arms. Did we want to back out? No way. We had been called by God to go to Japan. Our ship would be sailing soon. The strike was over. We knew in our hearts that God would take care of us. We were ready to go.

Tim, now nine months old, started talking in those days at the Home of Peace. Our freight was on the ship so we used harnesses to keep the children safe. During our extensive traveling, Tim had been kept in his drawer and the harness for such a long time that his walking was slow, but he could crawl and get into places that he wasn't supposed to be.

One of my classmates at CBC had promised to keep Tim in clothes during the five years we were to be away. He was one very handsome little guy and brought so much joy to his mother, father, and sister.

CHAPTER 14

Ship Ahoy

Go therefore and make disciples of all the nations,
baptizing them in the name of the Father and
the Son and the Holy Spirit, teaching them to
observe all that I commanded you; and lo, I am
with you always, even to the end of the age.

—Matthew 28:19–20

In late April 1951, the first group set sail, and all of us at the
Home of Peace went to the docks to see them off. Freighters
were the least expensive way to cross the Pacific Ocean. Roger
recalled it would be easier the way he went to the South Pacific the
first time—flying his P-47 fighter. However, we were happy to go by
freighter.

Two weeks later, the second group took off, and in early May,
we shipped out with the Bests and the Blevins on the *F. J. Luckenbach*.
The cabins were really nice and large enough to feel at home. It was
different going on a ship since I had never been on one. The children
thought it was wonderful.

Slowly, the ship backed away from the dock. It was a rainy day
with gray skies. We each stood on deck and watched the ship slide
through the water. We watched as the Golden Gate Bridge slowly
came into view past the American flag flapping in the wind at the
head of the ship en route up the Alaska coastline before heading

south to Japan. The Korean War was starting up, and every day was important to our arrival in Japan.

One thing I learned in our first hour of the Pacific was that the ocean was very rough. One of the ship's crewmen made the remark that all of us would be pretty sick. I found out later what that meant, but thankfully, the rough seas didn't seem to bother the children. They were raring to go each day. Roger was so sick every day. We would think it would be better the next day, but it wasn't. He would have loved to be in the cockpit of his fighter than to be on the freighter.

There were no other passengers on board, just us six adults with six kids. It rained and stormed all day every day. The ship rocked from stem to stern, side to side, all day and night. The ship was not equipped with stabilizers.

I wish I could say the rain stopped and the ocean became quiet, but that didn't happen. If anything, it got worse. The attractions were vicious as far as seeing rough waters were concerned. You have never seen the fury of an ocean until you have been tossed on it for fourteen days from San Francisco to Yokohama, Japan. It was never quiet, and many days, the water went right over our ship as it rocked.

One night, as we were going to bed, we got the children settled, but the ship was rocking and rolling until we thought it might be the last night we would be alive. Roger, and I had climbed into our bunks, and I called up to him, "Honey? Can I come up to your bunk? If I die on this ocean, I want to go in your arms."

I heard him chuckle then he gave me his hand to help me up. As we snuggled in bed that night after our usual prayer time, we both had peace that all was going to be all right. We would arrive in Japan safely because that was God's will.

We had peace that we were on that ship by God's grace, and He was taking us through the storm, in the storm and on very rough seas. We had been called of God to go. We wondered if the water was as rough for Jonah when he was in the belly of the whale.

Early in our trip, we made friends with some of the ship's crew. Our steward was a wonderful gentle man who loved kids. He often came to our room to play with Linda and Tim and to read to them.

He was a family man who missed his own children. We appreciated his care and concern.

Sydney and Dorothy Best and their three sons had served in China for some years and were older than the rest of us. Sydney was British, and his loving wife served tea and biscuits every day right on time. Dick and Claudia Blevins were there with daughter Jennifer, who was school-age. With three children of school-age, Dorothy had material, and we decided to have school each day. We moms did the teaching while the dads took care of the children who were not quite ready for school.

While the children played and napped, we adults at other times read the five books we were to read before we reached Japan. We learned a great deal about the country but could have learned more about "people skills," how to live overseas. We also learned a great deal about each other. Prayer time and Bible time was so important. I was grateful for all the good lessons we were learning.

Mealtime was not the greatest for everyone, but it was delicious and a great variety. Those of us who did not lose it after each meal enjoyed it all the time.

One morning, the captain announced that we were going to be crossing the International Date Line, and he asked if we wanted a second Friday or a second Saturday. Our menu was fish on Friday and steak on Saturday. We all opted for steak, and it was delicious.

Finally, the captain told us that we would be in Yokohama harbor the next morning. The sight of land was surreal. We had seen water, water, and water for fourteen days. We packed up our suitcases and waited for that wonderful time to disembark. We thanked the crew for their many kindnesses. Customs officials came out to meet the ship to carry on business with the captain. We could see the docks, and in the dim light of the docks, we could see some of our coworkers who arrived earlier had assembled to meet us. What a happy sight it was seeing the Fosters, Dillons, and Reasoners.

We saw a billboard not too far away from the dock. We were excited that we could read the katakana word, *ta-ba-ko*. The billboard was advertising tobacco. All of our memorizing of the Japanese alphabet during our trip across the Pacific allowed us to read the word "tobacco." We were excited that we could read and knew what we had read, and it was funny just the same.

There were many workers on the dock in straw capes and pointed straw hats to keep the rain off their bodies, running from one end of the dock to the other. Each was carrying some part of our baggage to its destination. We tried to thank them, but at that point, our vocabulary consisted of *ta-ba-ko*.

One of our senior missionaries could say it for all of us. He had been in Japan for a few years. We all thought, "We will be able to say that one of these days."

I don't think any of us thought it would take so long to be able to converse in Japanese. We soon were going to find out what it was going to take to be able to actually talk and teach in the new language, but by God's grace, it would happen.

CHAPTER 15

Getting Settled in Our New Homeland

And we know that God causes all thing to work together for good to those who love God, to those who are called according to His purpose.

—Romans 8:28

There we were in Japan, a country that not too many years earlier had been our enemy in war. But by the grace of God, we were going to be calling this country "home" for the next five years. Little did we realize all of the events that were to follow. But we were in Japan to serve our Lord Jesus. We knew we had been called, and we had His peace that we were there to do the work He had called us to do.

The next leg of our journey was a long and bumpy car ride from Yokohama to a place called Higashikurume. Our eyes were weary at three in the morning. We tried hard to see what we could of our new homeland. Trees were trees, but people were people. They were the reason we had come. So many things mulled through my mind as I watched the rain pelt the windshield. I listened to the chatter in the car and watched our children sleeping in our laps. It was a very exciting time and one I shall never forget.

I don't recall how long the trip took from Yokohama to Higashikurume, but it was long and damp, and we were all tired. We were greeted with more hellos on the compound we'd call home.

FEGC had purchased a piece of property as a site for evangelism in Higashikurume that previously was a dairy farm for the emperor. Later, several mission organizations agreed that a training site was necessary to train Japanese pastors and workers. The site became the Japan Bible Institute (JBI). The property had several buildings that had been barns for the cows. They were suitable for the cows but not for classrooms, so modifications needed to be completed. Other buildings were modified for living and studying conditions.

When we were taken to our abode, we had a huge room over the "ice" house, with a machine that was noisily still working. We had a small room off the large room, and a kitchen divided our apartment with the Browns. We shared the kitchen and bathroom that had a flush toilet and a huge bathtub—luxury exemplified. A bunk bed graced our wall and a small table with a tiny lovely bouquet sat in the middle of the table.

This was our first home in Japan, and it was wonderful. We knelt together and thanked Jesus for our safety on the rough ocean and on the bumpy road from the dock in Yokohama. Roger lifted Tim into the top bunk and crawled in beside him. Linda and I curled up together in the lower bunk. We were all so grateful to be settled in for our first "night," which was morning in Japan.

Time-wise, our heads were messed up after crossing so many time zones from San Francisco to Japan. We were awakened about 7:00 a.m. Japan time, scurried out of bed, dressed, and were escorted to the dining room. I will always recall our first breakfast—rice. Each of the adults had chopsticks, and the children had spoons. Rice was the main food that summer. It was tasty and filling, and our chopstick skills improved with each meal. When we could clean our bowls of the rice, we had arrived. It took two or three meals to accomplish that feat.

We more or less had the weekend to do what needed to be done. Roger and I made friends with Ted and Ellen Bollman through the mail and were happy to actually meet. They had a jeep, and we went off to order a "*futon*" that first day. We didn't know what a "*futon*" was, but we knew it was going to be our bed. The bunks were fine, but when we learned what a *futon* was, we knew it would be better.

Our futon was a thick-padded, extralong double-bed-sized pad that we folded up each morning and stored in a closet.

Every evening, it was taken out and laid out for a bed. We had pillows, sheets, and blankets in our drums, but they hadn't arrived yet. We borrowed several blankets from Ellen. Tim's play bed and drawer bed was with our freight, which was to arrive in a week or so. So living out of our suitcases soon was a conversation topic as we laughed over what we had brought and what we had put in the drums.

That first weekend went all too fast. Most of us had sea legs that needed encouragement. Our sleep time was so confused, but we finally, bit by bit, adjusted to the time difference.

We knew Saturday that we were going to start language study and the beginning of orientation on Monday. We had all read our books that we were to have read, and we knew basically the material in the books. We had all memorized the alphabet and could recognize hiragana and katakana. Hiragana was Japanese scattered throughout kanji, and katakana was written to tell foreign words— i.e., sweater=*setta*.

Monday morning, we traipsed down the stairs, turned our children over to Kobayashi san, a dear young girl who would be taking care of Danny Brown, Sarah Reasoner, and our Tim, as well as our other children. She made sure they were fed and played with and napped. We trusted her. They played and seemed to have a great time, rain or shine.

We were pretty exhausted that first day as jet lag was still with us. We really wanted to sleep. That night, we all had a good night's sleep. The next day was more of the same routine—language study, orientation, supper, and to bed.

As the adults settled in for language study and orientation, our days were pretty full. We had three teachers, who I thought were really old ladies, but they were only in their forties. Their Japanese kimonos tightly wrapped around their bodies made them look older. We were all eager to learn Japanese, and they were thrilled with us when there was some success.

We were in three groups. Each teacher had a group of us, and after an hour, we would switch to the second teacher, then again an hour later to the third teacher. Halfway in the morning, we had tea and salty rice crackers called *sembe*. The tea was green, with no sugar added. The tea break was good and gave us the opportunity to check on the children and to run to the bathroom.

I recall one day during our tea break, I ran to our apartment to check on the children and found they were out for a walk. As I opened the door to go upstairs, I was greeted by water pouring down the stairs. I quickly ran up the stairs to find out the source of the leak. The water was coming from the kitchen sink pouring onto the floor, running through the closet where we stored our futon before cascading down the stairs.

I turned off the kitchen faucet and found it was full of Danny diapers. I also found dirty diapers in the toilet and in the bathtub as well. Our neighbor had gotten waylaid in the morning chores in her apartment and forgot to turn off the water. As quickly as I could, I ran back to class and called Dorothy, and the two of us worked for some time until we finally got the mess cleaned up.

It was rainy season, so hanging things up to dry was next to impossible. We had to make a place to dry things. The kids bedding had not gotten wet, but it took days for our futon to dry out. I can laugh about it today, but it sure wasn't funny at the time.

Roger made friends with a carpenter, Nojima san, and he designed a high chair that when was made, Sara and Tim could sit side by side with a spoon in each hand. Kobayashi san fed them, and when they were finished, she fed Danny or vice versa. It was really cute to see how she maneuvered all three children so all got something to eat. She was a lovely young woman, and we were so glad she was there for our children. She took them for walks, and they loved that too.

We were all eager to learn Japanese. We all wanted to talk to the people, to tell them about Jesus. We all knew that the only way we would be able to do that was to study to get the language. It had been said that Japanese was and is the hardest language in the world to learn. Of course, the Japanese will say English is the hardest to learn.

All of my high school study in Latin, French, and Spanish growing up was nothing like learning to read and write Japanese.

It rained steadily the first couple of weeks, but the rain sure didn't keep us from doing what needed to be done. By the end of the first couple of weeks, our teachers had us pegged as to who was doing well and who was not. We then were divided into classes A, B, or C. Roger did very well. I did poorly but kept at it. The struggle of everyday living and language school with three hours in the afternoon were stressful months. Keeping priorities in the right order was not easy.

We did note that there was a large circular cemented area—about twenty-five feet in diameter—that had been used as a walking circle for the emperor's dairy cows. It was a great place to set up a volleyball court. Someone found a ball and net, and we had a great time batting that ball over the net and playing several games of volleyball after supper.

Roger and Rollie really kept things humming on the court. Those who didn't play were noisy cheer makers. Others watched the children, but all had a great time. My hands were so sore from my skin problems that playing volleyball was really hard for me. However, I sure could cheer them on as they played. In those early days, we developed friendships that lasted a lifetime.

That cow-walking circle also housed a bug called a *buyo*, a vicious little gnat that bit bare legs and caused huge welts that swelled up almost twice the size of a normal leg. We had never seen anything like it. Many of us suffered those months while we played volleyball.

The kanji characters reminded me of classes where I had shorthand when I went to night school while I was working for my dad in Baltimore.

Kore wa hon des. Kore wa empitsu des. Kore wa mannenhitsu des. These sentences were repeated over and over. We knew "This is a book," "This is a pencil," "This is a fountain pen," *Are mo empitsu des*—this too is a pencil and so forth.

Dorothy was a pro when it came to learning Japanese. Her ability to concentrate was amazing when all around her would be chaos.

We had many good laughs as we had many funny things happen living in the icehouse where our apartments were located.

The fumes from the icehouse were overwhelming one night, and all of us staggered out the door and knocked on our neighbor's door. Bob and Dorothy welcomed us in, and we stayed until the fellows could get the carbon monoxide fumes cleared out. We were a motley crew wrapped in blankets, carrying Tim and Danny. Linda wasn't happy to have been wakened early that morning, but we all managed.

We were fortunate to have running water and flush toilet. Others had to use an outhouse and pump at one end of the property. One morning, we heard Dick cry out, "My wallet just fell in the outhouse!" It looked like it was a goner, but he did manage to fish it out with a long pole. It smelled awful. It took some time until he got it cleaned up enough to be able to use it again.

Ted, Ellen, Roger and I, and our children enjoyed Ted's jeep, and we loved going to see some of the sights of Japan. One day, we set off to find the orphanage that Roger and his army buddy Dub Jackson had helped get off the ground in 1945.

We wanted to find Miss Francis, Mrs. Dievendorf, Betty Kilburn, and Honichi san, whom the fellows had met during their war days. That was five years earlier and everything had changed since then. People were living under any train trestles that had some dry areas. It was beyond my way of thinking to see dozens of people sleeping on the ground and eating by a *konro* (*hibachi*-style cook stove). Area after area was burned out. There were masses of people everywhere. Trains were packed moving a crowd from one area to the next.

We kept going up one street and down another until something looked familiar. There were no street signs, only things like a rock pile, a row of trees—anything that Roger could recall.

Suddenly Roger called out, "Turn here." We did and went up a steep hill for blocks. Whoops, turn here, and there were a few houses untouched by fire. There were some children playing in the street. Honichi san came to the door when she saw Roger; she threw her arms around him—not Japanese style at all—and we had a royal welcome.

She said she thought she would never see him again when he left the last time. Oh, the welcome as we sat on the floor and listened as they chatted about the old days. Between Honichi san's broken English and Roger's childlike Japanese, they were able to communicate.

She served tea, and we met the orphans. Several were older fellows and had gone to work, but there still were some young children who had lived there since the war ended. The home wasn't anything fancy. It was a home for children who had lost their parents. Honichi san loved them and shared her life with them and told them about Jesus. She had come to know the Lord through the witness of Miss Francis when they were interned during the war.

A couple of the boys came home from work and were so happy to see Roger. They had been young boys when Roger and Dub found them wandering on the streets and brought them to Honichi san. I had only heard about the orphanage, but seeing it in action was such a joy. It was so good to hear those two young men tell of their love for Jesus. It still brings tears of joy thinking about those memories.

Another time, Ted took us all to see fireworks on the river. It was a beautiful evening, and there were large groups of people sitting on the riverbanks to watch the lovely display of every kind of firework in so many different colors. The *oohs* and *ahs* sent chills through us as we were slowly becoming part of Japanese life. We fell into bed each night weary from all the activities of the day.

After we had been in language school for several months, we were encouraged to prepare our testimony in Japanese, or at least a brief message that we could share in a church someplace. We found there were Japanese who gathered in a school or some such place of worship to the true God.

One Sunday, we went to a large building that resembled an airplane hangar. The teacher asked if any of us sang. Roger told the teacher that I did, and I was volunteered to sing a solo. I picked "The Old Rugged Cross," and it was translated into Japanese for me. That was my first solo in Japanese but certainly not my last.

Over our time in Japan, there were several songs that became standard favorites for us. Below are several that have been translated. The first line are the words in Japanese, the second line is the translation of the Japanese words into English.

"For God So Loved the World"

Kami wa yobito wo aishitamou
God loves the people of the world
Waga sukui wa ju-jika ni ari
Our salvation is in the Cross
Yagate Shu Iesu wa kitaritamou
Someday, the Lord Jesus will come
Nantaru ai zo
What kind of love is that?!

"Jesus Loves Me"

Shu ware wo aisu, Shu was tsuyokereba
The Lord loves me. If the Lord is strong
Ware yowakutomo, Osore wa araji
Even if I am weak, I have nothing to fear.

Chorus

Waga Shu Iesu, Waga Shu Iesu
My Lord Jesus, My Lord Jesus,
Waga Shu Iesu, Ware wo aisu
My Lord Jesus, He loves me.
Waga tsumi no tame, Sakae wo sutete
For my sins, He threw glory away
Ame yori kudari, Ju-jika ni tsukeri
He came down from Heaven to be put on the Cross.
Mikuni no kado wo, Hirakite ware wo
He opened the gates of Heaven

Maneki tamaeri, Isamite noboran.
And invited us in. Let's climb up quickly.
Waga Kimi Iesu yo, Ware wo kiyomete
My Lord Jesus! Cleanse me
Yoki hataraki wo, Nasashime tamae
May you empower to do a good work.

"Hallelu, Hallelu, Hallelujah"

Hareru, hareru, hareruya, Shu wo homeyo
Hallelu, Hallelu, Hallelujah, Praise ye the Lord
Hareru, hareru, hareruya, Sambishiyo
Hallelu, Hallelu, Hallelujah, Let's praise Him

I found it easier to sing in Japanese than to speak the language. It was such a joy to be able to share God's Word, even as simple as the message might have been, and the people listened so carefully.

Another trip we took was up to the mountains. Roger had prepared a message with lots of Bible verses, but we had an interpreter who just wanted to learn English and left out many things as Roger spoke. That day, we knew we were going to have to learn the language or die trying. He said, "I don't want to be tied to someone else to speak for me." It gave us a strong incentive to study like nothing else did.

The three plus months of language study and orientation came to a dull thud end. Ted had been looking for houses for the sixteen families who had arrived that spring. It was like trying to find the proverbial needle in the haystack. There were some people who didn't want Americans living in their homes, but that was rare to hear.

Johnny and Anna Siebert looked at a house in Kori. Rollie and Esther Reasoner looked at one in Utsunomiya. Conrad and Ruth Miller still were single at that time and would not be able to marry for at least a year after they arrived in Japan. Sydney and Dorothy Best moved to Chinatown in Yokohama. The others found just the right place to live that a church could be planted in the near future.

Village life sure was different from city life, and we were all excited about moving to our own place of work.

Yes, we had to finish language study. That meant finding a teacher to help us finish books 1, 2, 3, and 4. Exams followed each section. It was wonderful to see it all come together in our study. Some folks learned well, found good teachers, and were at ease with the language.

Roger was excited one day to find he was speaking Japanese and hadn't thought about what he was saying. It took me nearly two years, but one day, it hit me that I hadn't thought about what I was saying, but it was being said in Japanese.

CHAPTER 16

Hachioji: Our First Assignment

For it is by grace you have been saved, through faith; and that not of yourselves, it is the gift of God; not as a result of works, so that no one can boast.

—Ephesians 2:8–9

In August 1951, with three steel drums, a trunk, our futon, a fold-up picnic table and benches, washing machine, and two children with weary parents, we moved to our new home in Hachioji, a city that had been almost completely leveled five years earlier and now had a population of about 150,000. During the war, US planes had been ordered to drop any leftover bombs from their original mission on Hachioji.

We were the only English-speaking Americans anywhere around. Moving to Hachioji meant we were all on our own. We didn't know how the people in the city would feel about having Americans in their midst. We were so new to Japan so soon after the war, that I was afraid of being pushed in front of a train speeding into Hachioji station. It was not long before we were relieved of our concerns.

Many people in those early days lived in corrugated tin houses, under train trestles—anywhere to find shelter—but our home in Hachioji was a lovely home by Japanese standards. It had been built right after the war to replace one that had been destroyed by fire-bombs dropped during the war.

The landlord, Sugigaki san, had contracted tuberculosis and had moved into a sanitarium to treat his disease, so his home was put up for rent, and his wife and daughter moved in with her in-laws next door. Sugigaki san had contacted Ted Bollman, and after seeing the house, Ted thought it would be perfect for the Fox family and signed the papers to rent it for us.

We fell in love with it the first time we saw it. It would be perfect for our family of four. Glass arcadia-style windows were on the south side, and there was a high fence across the front with a *mon* (gate) to walk through. The doors on the gate slid on a rail and were closed tightly at night with a bar so no one could get in.

Our trash collection was a hole in the ground where we burned everything, and when it was full, we dug a new hole. Our bathroom was an indoor/outdoor traditional Japanese-style toilet located near the front door.

There was a slit in the floor, and users stood or squatted over the slit. Ours soon had a seat and cover built and installed so that the children and others would not fall into the "night soil." The smell, though, was terrible with or without the seat.

The bathing place was a wooden *ofuro* (bathtub) with a cast-iron box at one end. We heated the water by burning wood in the firebox. We learned during orientation that you scrubbed up and rinsed off outside of the *ofuro*, then got in to soak and relax when clean. We were able to at least get rid of the dusty sweat of summer, and we were warm at night without central heating in the winter.

It did take a bit of time to get the kitchen the way we wanted. It had been so black from burning charcoal for cooking that even with ten coats of white paint and one coat of red, it never did brighten the walls.

We obtained two bicycles, and Roger would strap Tim to his back, and Linda rode behind me. Sometimes we switched children, but we learned a lot about our new hometown just riding our bikes.

Shortly after we moved to Hachioji, Ted came to visit and told us about a military jeep that was for sale. Roger and Ted looked it over, and aside from not having a roof, doors, windshield, and with poor tires, it was all right. Roger said those were all things that could be taken care of. So for days, we could be found on the front side of the house working on the jeep. It needed to be in good working order before winter arrived.

Our training by Bernie while we were in college on engines, tires, etc. came back to us. We had worked on our Chevy, taking it apart and putting it back together through the night once to get it back on the road. We knew we could put the jeep in order.

However, finding sheet metal was a big question. Roger did find a bit of sheet metal at the airbase, enough to fashion a roof for the jeep. He also found sections of Plexiglas that we used for a windshield and windows. Parts of old jeeps at the airbase also provided things we needed to winterize our jeep.

Roger tried to find tires, but to no avail. One morning, he went out and found four flat tires on our jeep. However, God was in control and soon four good tires were provided.

Roger painted it blue. It was not showroom fresh but it ran. We bumped many miles over many roads as it served our needs very well.

After a few months in Hachioji, the one-week orientation we had had with R. E. Thompson in the states began to sink in.

- *Simplicity in our material things*
- *Adaptability to any change, and*
- *Discipline in being obedient to the study and will of the Word of God had been taught.*

I was so glad that we had been simple in "things" with which to cope. There had been so many changes from the day our last support came that adapting to changes in having and not having water or electricity. Seeing young people coming and going all seem to fit into adaptability. Discipline was the key to keeping on target as we clung to the Word of God.

We soon found that Sugigaki san's daughter and Linda would become fast friends. She taught Linda Japanese, and without my having a teacher, she acted as an interpreter when I needed help.

The family who lived to the left of us had seven children and a horse. The horse was first in at night so the family slept around it. I don't know who was the warmest. I do know it was a sad family when the mother died delivering the latest child. The whole neighborhood rallied around to care for the family, but it wasn't long before the father, the kids, and the horse moved away from the corrugated tin house to another place. Several of the children had, however, come to Christ in the first Sunday school that we had.

Linda turned four years old in July, and Tim had turned one. Tim had learned to walk while we were first in language school in Higashikurume and was quick as lightning when he wanted to be. Shoes are removed before entering Japanese houses, so we kept socks over his shoes while he was in the house so he would walk more easily, but it didn't slow him down.

There was a lovely park up the street from where we lived. In the spring, it was bordered with beautiful cherry trees that bloomed beautiful white and pink flowers in the spring with the beauty of Mount Fuji in the background. Cherry trees took on a new meaning to me.

Many years before, I had gone on a family picnic with my parents to see the cherry trees along the Potomac River in Washington, DC. Mother loved the see those trees in bloom. However, they were more beautiful in Japan. Japanese loved walking in this park. We joined in the walk to enjoy them too.

Our blond-haired children were touched and squeezed by passersby who stopped and asked to feel the blonde hair and white-skinned children. Linda and Tim were a bit skeptical of all the attention, but they endured it anyway. One of the first things we had been told during our orientation was that Japanese never show affection in public, and we should adhere to that policy as well. But that first time strolling through the park, we saw there was a lot of hand-holding and kissing by Japanese young people. We had to smile as we walked along.

I didn't dare go shopping without Roger at first because in some cases, I had no idea what was on the shelf. Rice was rationed, and we found our neighbors needed it more than we did, so we gave most of it to them. It was a delight to go into various stores and watch them wrap up our purchase maybe in newsprint or banana leaves tied with string or to have eggs carefully tucked in a leaf to be carried home.

Having to go to a liquor store to buy sugar and salt just about did us in. Paper goods were in another store. Toilet paper came in large flat bundles instead of rolls. Sandpaper was softer, or maybe pages from the Sears catalog or maybe even a corncob would be softer than that toilet paper. It was strange how "adaptability" can be a part of everyday life.

We built relationships by getting to know the mayor and other city officials. We learned to take a packet of postcards to the officials we met. We were welcomed by each official and served green tea at each meeting. They encouraged us to come back.

We began to develop friendships with the fishmonger, the meat man, a chicken keeper, the bread man, and the family who ran the vegetable store; even a tailor and his wife who lived along the train tracks waved as we went by. The policeman on the corner looked forward to a visit. The china shopkeeper really became a good friend. That was one of my favorite stopping places because of the variety of shapes and dishes of which I was so fond.

We found this wonderful fruit and vegetable store about twenty minutes from the house. The store carried pretty much the same things—onions, thin, skinny, foot-long carrots, cabbage, and *daikon* (a member of the turnip family).

One day, after about two years being in Hachioji, our vegetable man's daughter arrived and with a smile on her face, slid open the front door and called out, "*Gomen nasai*" (excuse me). When I arrived at the door, she handed me a package. "Sensei, my father was in the wholesale market yesterday in Tokyo and found a new vegetable and thought of you," she said.

I opened the package while sitting on my knees in the entryway and beheld the most beautiful cauliflower, the first I had seen since we left America. I offered the pay for the cauliflower, but she insisted that her father had bought it for me. Have you ever tried to make a cauliflower last for ten days for a family of four? We cherished and enjoyed it. In return, we baked some cookies to give to our vegetable man to show our gratitude.

Word spread about the cookies, for when I arrived one day at the bread store, I was surprised to see a group of ladies admiring a cake—well, at least it looked like a cake. It was covered in icing that was a finger thick, and the bread man was about to hand me a slice when a woman hurried into the store, and I heard her say, "The foreigner's baby is dead."

I quickly went out the door to where Tim had been soundly sleeping in the carriage by the door—he was still there to my joy— and I reached in and picked him up and laid him over my shoulder. He was far from dead, but I learned that day that Japanese never lay a baby or a toddler on its tummy face down for fear that the child would suffocate. Instead, they would use a wide piece of velvet called an *onbuhimo* to tie the child to their back. There was no neck support, and the child's head would hang behind its mother, head lolling back and forth while the mother walked.

When I assured the ladies that Tim was okay, all went back to normal. I ended up with the cake for my family to test. I may have been the bread store's biggest customer, and because we shared our rice ration, we did use bread a great deal. Roger often made bread for us, but this bread man's *pan* (bread) was delicious.

When I returned to his store, I was to let him know how the cake had tasted. That night, we hoped to have a wonderful dessert, but to our amazement, under the finger thick icing, there was a white cake. When we all bit into the cake, "ugh" was heard all around. How were we going to tell our friend the cake was awful? The icing was made from lard. It took us a while to get that taste out of our mouths.

The baker showed up at our door later in the week to find out if his first try at cake making and icing was a success. I took him into my kitchen, got out a dictionary and a recipe book, and we sat down together as I explained the ingredients of cake and icing. Dozens of tries later, he became known for his cakes and cookies, and I don't think anyone knew he had received instruction from a foreigner. We became good friends over the years.

Food became more plentiful over time too, and that was exciting because the allure of onions, skinny carrots, and oversized cabbages was waning. Little by little, we started seeing potatoes and yams on the market.

Vendors were a great attraction in the early days, and people would always respond to their calls of *yaki mo* (I have sweet potatoes), and children from far and near would run to buy a sweet potato for one yen or so and hurry back to their mother or to care for baby brother or sister.

We were never quite sure of the quality of the food or the cleanliness of the food, but when the *bakudan arare san* came, we would take our rice ration and the wheat grain that we had purchased and have it popped so that we could have puffed rice and puffed wheat for breakfast. It was a welcome change from the fish-fed eggs that we normally had for breakfast even with the evaporated milk we had gotten used to drinking.

Food reached a new level of interest when butter and cheese and milk came to market. There seemed to be many new and different foods to try, and those were fun experiences. It was not long that we noticed that Japanese children's teeth no longer looked like a hacksaw had been at them because new teeth came in and were not rotting away as had been the case earlier. Adults with gold fillings had them replaced with enamel and used the gold fillings to make rings again for their wives who had given them up during the war.

Over time, I found Japan a country of contrasts. It was a place where the woman was only to be seen in the home to serve her family rice, then retreating back into the kitchen to eat alone. But women also were the street cleaners. When roads started getting paved, it was the women, covered head to toe to keep the sun away or to keep warm, who carried the load of cement from one place to another. It was the grandmothers who carried large bags of black market rice on their backs. It was the woman who kept the money in order, paid the bills, and saved for the future. It was the woman who saw to it that her sons and daughters attended the proper schools to get the best education so they could get the best job possible so they could take care of the elderly.

It was the woman who kept things together, knowing perhaps her husband had a concubine and arrived home late at night and left early in the morning to earn enough to take care of his family and his "friend." It was the woman who kept the house clean, shopped three times a day for food to put meals on the table, and who waited on her husband from the minute he walked in the door until he left the next day.

It was a man's world, but it was the woman that made things happen and keep things moving. Because the women were hard workers at all sorts of things and were home, it was easier to reach them to share the good news of God's Word.

Living in Japan, we saw many changes as the country grew out of the destruction of World War II. Early on, we would see people walking or riding bicycles everywhere. It was not unusual to see people riding on bikes with a family of six on one bike or a basket full of baby goats tied on the back or a tower of stools tied to the back of the bike. Our children had fun counting all the things they saw tied on the back of a bicycle when they passed.

Small restaurants sometimes would deliver food orders, and a *demaemochi* (delivery person) would deliver the food on a tray while riding a bicycle. We never saw one lose their balance, though there were times we thought they would. Anything you wanted delivered could be delivered on bicycles. Then came the *rea* (a three-wheeled cart) that was attached to the back of a bicycle that made delivery much easier, except for the man pedaling the bike because the loads became larger and larger.

There were cabs in Hachioji. They weren't the greatest looking taxis, but they got you where you wanted to go. All were powered by charcoal in those early days. Due to severe shortages of gasoline, many civilian vehicles—cars, trucks, even motorcycles—were converted to operate on gases generated from burning coal or wood. Flammable gases were routed to a carburetor of sorts, mixed with air, and burned in the engine's combustion chambers. As a result, soot covered, well, everything.

Buses then made their appearance and then trucks and then a wonderful invention came with the motorized bicycle, then motorcycles in all sizes. Competition from automobile makers—Honda, Toyota, Datsun, and Mitsubishi—filled the market with cars, and each was trying to build a better car than a competitor.

We were the objects of a lot of curiosity. It seemed that at least once a week, we would have a beggar at the door seeking a hand-out. In freezing weather, they would come barefoot begging from the American. It was good to have a tract on hand with the food or little money we could spare. I recall that early in our years on the field, a woman came to the door with her little girl, and it appeared that the girl was mute. I felt sorry for the two of them standing there in the cold, and I asked them to come in.

I tried to talk to that woman all day, offered her food and green tea, but she would not partake of a thing. I thought at the time she was mute, but our neighbor reassured me that she was not. When the morning passed and afternoon was fading and the evening was coming, she made a move to get up. I could not believe that I had been sitting on my knees all day. I questioned my ability to stand, but I did. She bowed low and departed with a tract and a bag of cookies for the little girl.

Two weeks later, I discovered that she was sort of a spy for the neighborhood and was there to see how much patience I had. I never saw her again, but from that day on, the neighbors were friendlier. I guess I passed that particular test as far as they were concerned.

We always said the street we lived on was Cherry Street. I don't know if that was the real name for the street, but it was lined for many blocks with cherry trees. A stonecutter was located on the corner of our street. So when anyone came to visit, we told them to turn left at the street where the bakery was, then go up a hill through the cherry trees and turn right at the corner, where the stone cutter was located, then go past the park until you see a tall fence and gate that slid open, and then come in the front yard. It was easy to find if you followed instructions.

One day, we were eating lunch, and we heard a loud voice in English say, "Does Roger Fox live in this neighborhood?"

We left our table and ran out the gate to find Lt. Chuck Pressor, a friend of ours from CBC days, along with an interpreter. They had driven all over the city, and someone had said that Americans lived in the Daimachi area. Chuck had some time with us and after a good visit, headed back to Tokyo. He later returned to Korea, where he was stationed. Chuck and his family also went to the mission field following his time in the army.

Hachioji is located west of Tokyo and has a long history. Its beginning was the foundation of a medieval fortress, named *hachioji*, for eight legendary young princes, each guarding one of the ancient Japanese gods. We were in a city that also had eight Buddhist temples, and as far as I knew, there were no Christians, no English speakers to talk to, so our conversations were limited to our family.

Hachioji also was a silk-weaving town. You could walk around and hear the loom shuttles at work. Most anytime of the day, looms for making silk material were clicking away. After his treatment at the tuberculosis sanitarium, our landlord moved into a house that had four apartments in front, and all were used for weaving. The silk worms nested in their attic. When I visited my friend Sugigaki san, I could hear the worms chewing. It was a most interesting sound, like the rustling of lots of loose paper.

We were a curiosity but for the most part felt very wanted. Rarely did someone pass us on the street without saying, "*Ohiogozaimasu*" (good morning) or something else we understood. Everyone knew where the Americans lived, and they knew a great deal about us as we found out as we became more fluent in Japanese.

Living in Japan those early days was so different than what we were used to in America. The rainy season was almost more than we could bear. Winter was cold and wet. Snow fell and melted by midday, leaving ankle-deep mud. Paved roads were unknown. During the winter, it was as cold inside as it was outside. The paper walls didn't keep much out. The attic was a gymnasium for the rats, which scurried hither and yon on the ceiling, entertaining us morning through night. They had a habit of coming down into the house at night, causing me to fear that the children would be bit.

It wasn't long until strange places became common. The smells were part of everyday life, and we learned to live with them. We learned to adapt to ankle-deep mud, the stares, the strange food, and the cold damp winters and steamy hot summers.

One Sunday, we were enjoying some fun as a family when we heard new voices. It was a freezing day, and these girls were calling, "Is anyone home?"

We called out for them to come in as we reached the door. Two teachers from a nearby US airbase were standing in our entranceway. We invited them to come in, and they stepped up the high step into the living room by our hibachi charcoal pit. They sat on *zabuton* (flat cotton cushions) that we had for guests and held their hands over the charcoal urn to get warm. They didn't stay very long because they were so cold. We didn't have heat in the house other than our hibachi, and we were wearing *tangens* (padded kimonos). We were warm, but they were cold. They had driven out and assured us they'd be back sometime.

Sometime came that next Sunday when they arrived with a large carefully wrapped gift. Upon coming into the house, they handed us the package that we opened with joy because it was a wonderful new electric blanket. They explained that we could all sit under it, and it could be over us while we slept.

We were very grateful and thanked them over and over. It lasted a long time and was a welcome gift for the family. What they had not known was that the blanket worked great as long as we had electricity. Sometimes at night, electricity was off, but we enjoyed it when we did have electricity.

CHAPTER 17

Meg's Japanese

For you have need of endurance, so that when you have done the will of God, you may receive what was promised.

—Hebrews 10:36

We continued our language study after we moved to Hachioji. Roger and I found a distinguished gentleman who was the vice principal of a local high school. He came and taught us every day. I struggled, but Roger kept going. He enjoyed meeting with and learning from this man and studied hard to be able to use the language. We had spent nearly a year learning the language.

One day, some neighbors were on the street visiting. I thought it would be good to go out and see how they were doing and to practice my Japanese. As I approached and bowed, they bowed and then snickered. I hated that because it had become a way of life for me. I didn't know why they would laugh. Was it because I was taller than they, was not Japanese, my children were blonde, or we did have a jeep not much better than a buckboard? "Why are you laughing?" I finally asked that day.

The women started laughing even harder, hiding their mouths behind their hands. Finally, my closest friend said, "They are laughing because you are speaking men's Japanese."

I went in the house crying. Why wouldn't I speak that way? I had a man for a teacher, and we thought all Japanese was the same. Then we learned that there was the crudeness of men's Japanese, polite Japanese, women's Japanese, children's Japanese, and then, as a coworker chimed in one day, "There is Meg's Japanese."

I was discouraged that day, for I had studied so hard to get the language and had claimed over and over the verses of Deuteronomy— "The cause that is too hard for you, bring it unto me and I will hear it." That was my language battle.

Years later, one of my dear Japanese friends said to me, "You may not speak perfect Japanese, but we know you love us and want us to know Jesus in our hearts."

Our language teacher came every day, five days a week. I was so happy that Roger learned the language so quickly because that meant that at least one of us could communicate with the people we met.

Many mornings we did have electricity, but I always had fresh water in the teapot over the *konro* (charcoal stove). It worked well enough to give us hot water for tea and dishes. One morning, I had not been prepared. There was no electricity, and the water went off when the electricity went off. I had no water and knew it was a poor thing to not serve tea to *sensei*.

What to do? After thinking a bit, I had been told that the front part of the *ofuro* (bath) had a section that always had clean water. I believed that story and went to the tub room and drew out water into my teapot, lit the charcoal, fanned it to get the fire going, and put the teapot on to boil. It took a bit of time, but the water finally got hot enough to make tea. I made my green tea and took it and two cups on a tray and served Roger and *sensei* (teacher) tea. Roger sputtered and swallowed, "There's soap in the water."

We could talk in English, and I was so embarrassed, but sensei was delighted, or was a perfect gentleman, and said it was the best tea he had ever had, then asked for a second cup. I felt terrible knowing that it tasted like soap, and rest assured, that never happened again. The teapot always had fresh water and was always hot by the time sensei came.

Language study was important to both of us. We decided that I needed to go to a school. We found a Lutheran language school for missionaries. I walked to and from the train station twenty to twenty-five minutes each way and rode to school about an hour away. It wasn't my favorite thing to do, but I was determined to learn Japanese, and I did make friends with other missionaries at the school.

I always tried to get on the train in the same place so that when I got off in the city of Ochanomizu, I would be near to the school so on cold days, I wouldn't have to walk as far. I enjoyed watching the other passengers. I was head and shoulders taller than anyone on the train, so I was stared at from head to toe. Being a foreigner on a train fully occupied by Japanese was scary at first, but the Lord was good and helped quiet down my fears, and I learned to enjoy each day of travel.

At a station not far from our home, a gentleman traveler would board the train with his clothes slung over his arm. He wore long underwear and his shoes were clipped over his fingers. He carried a cloth *furoshiki* (a large square piece of cloth used for carrying things). He opened the *furoshiki* and proceeded to get dressed in front of everyone in the train car. He then put his shoes in the *furoshiki* and tied the four corners together, sat down, opened his newspaper and enjoyed the rest of the trip. I did try with some success to learn new vocabulary as I traveled, so the time passed quickly.

Another stop on down the line brought another traveler carrying a stool and a newspaper. He boarded and used his stool on the very crowded train car while reading his newspaper. Roger and I coined a phrase for times like this—"different is different, not necessarily wrong."

Babies were strapped on mother's backs, old women with huge bundles of rice strapped to their heads, sometimes a young goat in a basket of a traveler—these were all not-too-unusual things I saw while riding the train. Sometimes I found some yen that I would pick up and hand to a passenger. Sometimes I would have to stand all the whole way to school, and other days I would be offered a seat. It wasn't much different going home, but many slept going home with me on the train. Once in a while, a weary traveler would rest his or her head on my shoulder as we rode along.

Many train rides, we saw older women carrying bundles of rice on their backs. Straps were pulled over their foreheads to keep them from slipping off. Roger learned early that if he gave up his seat on a train so the women with the rice bundle could sit down, she would step aside and let a child or a man take the seat he had made available.

I attended the school for just one year. The school was having financial difficulties and closed, but my "women's" Japanese had improved.

CHAPTER 18

Adjusting to Change

Do not fear, for I am with you;
Do not anxiously look about
you, for I am your God.
I will strengthen you, surely I will help you,
Surely I will uphold you with
My righteous right hand.

—Isaiah 41:10

Our life in Hachioji was different but normal compared to our lives in the states. Once in a while, Chuck Pressor would drive to our house in his jeep, where he could get away from work without being bugged. He would fall asleep on the *tatami* (straw mats) floor, and we would just close the *shoji* (rice-paper-covered doors) and let him sleep.

I struggled with the thought of having to have a maid in the house. I wasn't interested in having a maid, for I could take care of the house and kids. The house was clean, and the kids had clean clothes to wear as our small washing machine did get lots of use. But we found through trial and error that it was important to have someone in the house at all times to keep potential burglars away.

So we looked for a maid, someone who loved children and was willing to learn to clean an American home and who was willing to teach me how to take care of a Japanese home. They went together.

Several knew we were looking for someone, and an older lady along with a younger lady came to the door, opened our sliding door and called out, "*Gomen kurasai*" (may we come in, please?).

We invited them in, and with dictionary in hand, we talked and negotiated for the younger of the two to work as our maid. Michiko san seemed very pleasant and seemed happy with Linda and Tim. Michiko san was a very special young woman and became a good friend. We started calling her Mickey, and the name stuck.

I thought she was in her early twenties but found out a few days later that she was just sixteen. As all Japanese girls did at that time, she finished through grade six and then was to find a job. Her parents wanted her to learn English so that she could get a job at the air force base. Her sisters and brothers were all school teachers, and all lived with or near their parents. We learned the term "keeper of the bag" from Mickey. Her mom was keeper of the bag. The five children gave her all their paychecks and Mom doled out what each needed for the week in food, travel, clothes, etc. The rest was banked at the post office to grow until there was enough to have their own home so that they could get married.

Mickey came to work at 8:00 a.m. and left for home around 5:00 p.m. She did much of our shopping because she knew where to go for fruit and vegetables, if there was any in the stands. She knew where to buy salt and sugar. She knew where to find the freshest tofu in the morning.

The tofu man had a daughter who was Mickey's age. She started coming to one of the evening Bible classes that Roger taught. Makamura san was a darling girl and also became a good friend. She also asked Jesus into her heart. In time, she worked alongside us. Several years later, she went home to be with the Lord.

CHAPTER 19

Akitoshi and Yoneko Tahara's Story

Therefore if anyone is in Christ, he is a new creature; behold, the old things passed away; new things have come.

—2 Corinthians 5:17

One day, in 1951, the sliding sound of the *genkan* (entrance way door) caused us to realize we had a guest. "Dozo irashai," we called out. "Please come in."

In stepped a young Japanese man who inquired of the missionary (Roger), "Sensei, can you come to our night class in drama and criticize our work in English?"

"I'm sorry," Roger told him. "I can't do that. I do not know much about drama, but I'd like to talk to you about something of importance."

The dictionary finger was sore from trying to communicate that way, but Tahara san entered the guest room to hear more. Roger went through the colors of the wordless book that night as they talked about Jesus—black is sin, red is the blood of Jesus, white is a clean heart, gold is the promise of heaven, and green to grow strong and firm in the Lord like a tree.

The second time Tahara san came around, he said, "Yes, Jesus, I sinner, clean my heart and enter this heart now. Thank you. Amen."

Tahara san came back night after night following his night classes to learn more about Jesus and he became a member of our team.

A couple of years later, Robin and Willene McLeroy, another missionary family, moved to Hachioji near to us. Robin's language teacher came to him one night very upset because one of his favorite high school students had attempted to commit suicide by stepping in front of a train. She was alive but barely. Her legs were gone below the knee; her left arm was about gone and only had two fingers and a thumb left on her right. The attempt occurred several months earlier, and she had been recuperating in a local hospital, but she still was angry and still wanted to die.

The young teacher said, "You go to her. You have message to share. I won't listen, but she needs your message."

We learned that she had been so despondent over the death of her mother, who had been a devout follower of Shinto Buddhism. Following the weeks after her mother's death, she only went to school, went home, or went out all hours of the night with her friends in a continuous downward cycle of self-destruction. Finally, she thought, there was no reason to live.

Robin and Tahara san went to the hospital to see her. That first visit didn't go well as Robin and Tahara san left with her screaming, "I don't want to listen to you. Get out so I can die!"

The weeks that followed led to much prayer within our small group of believers as we prayed for this young high school student to find Jesus as well as to be able to function somehow, someway.

During a special Easter service, our friend Shelton Allen, who was fluent in Japanese, spoke in the church in our home, and Roger recorded that message. The next day, Robin and Tahara san arrived at the hospital with tape recorder and message in hand. Shelton's words were for a girl not only with a mutilated body but also with a broken heart.

As she listened to the message, she cried out to God to forgive her and to help her live for Him. "In Christ," she found she could share Jesus by writing notes with three fingers and holding paper with her stump. Soon after she was released to go home, she found she could cook, sew, mend, iron, clean, and in time, ride on the back seat of a motorcycle to attend Bible study and prayer meetings, and on Sunday, church services. The key that opened the lock and gave her something to live for was "in Christ."

Our son Gary's arrival on Linda's eighth birthday, in July 1955, was at the same time as Yoneko san was a new babe in Christ. A few months after her surgery to fit her with prosthetic legs, she moved in with us for a while. There was the constant battle between the "must" and the "good things" to do. It was like having two babies to care for. Yoneko san and her injuries were far more exciting than taking care of a baby in diapers. They both learned to walk in those days—Gary at six months, Yoneko san for the second time at age seventeen. Then the discipleship set in. What a joy to see her growth in the Lord.

Tahara san and Yoneko san were married in our living room Christmas time 1957. That was such a joy. We will never forget going shopping with her the night before their wedding for some white socks for her wedding day to cover her feet. When the sales girl saw us coming, she thought that because it was cold and damp, that Yoneko san was our interpreter. When she found that we could converse freely in Japanese, she asked what we wanted. She had not realized that our friend was handicapped and asked us if the socks were to keep Yoneko san's feet warm or for looks. We snickered and told the salesgirl they were for looks. Yoneko san then told her that her feet never got cold and proceeded to tell the salesgirl her story. A flushed girl came back with a variety of socks, a pair was selected, paid for, and we went home.

The wedding was beautiful, and the Taharas went on to continue serving the Lord, as did their two beautiful daughters. Yoneko san's story was later written into a book and then later turned into a film. The movie was translated into several different languages and reached people for Christ all around the world.

CHAPTER 20

Working for Christ

For you have been called for this purpose, since
Christ also suffered for you, leaving you an example for you to follow in His steps, who committed
no sin, nor was any deceit found in His mouth.

—1 Peter 2:21

We were trying to find our way around Hachioji and praying about how to start a church from nothing. There
were no courses in college for that, just many classes
on established churches. Our church in Horatio, South Carolina,
already was established before the pastor left, and the church people
stopped gathering. It did grow again after God brought us to that
church.

We now read a lot in Acts and prayed that God would show us
how to move ahead and what to do in starting a brand-new church,
and He began a work in both of us. Those first two years in Hachioji,
we did a lot of work at Tachikawa Air Force Base.

There was a small Sunday school for the children, and Chaplain
Hartman was very friendly. Christian officers had started a Bible
study class, and Roger was the teacher. An airman's Bible study group
started, and I began teaching a Sunday school class. That winter,
Chaplain Hartman asked me to direct the upcoming Vacation Bible
School.

We were involved and saw kids in my class turn their hearts to Jesus. Airmen came to Christ and grew. Letting Christ lead his life changed Chaplain Hartman's life. His messages grew as he gave out the Word of God. Yes, the Lord blessed. The classes grew, and VBS was great.

It was exciting to sing in a quartet, to see chapel wives get started in a Christian life, to see so many come to the Lord. Some of those young men went on to pastor churches in America. And we still were having Japanese Bible classes nearly every night.

We were busy, content, and didn't have much time to think about why we were in Japan. On our calendars, I had put all the company we had go through our home. Five nights out of the five years in Hachioji, we were a family alone in our home. The rest of the time, we had VIPs, servicemen, and upcountry missionaries who needed a futon to sleep on when they traveled to Tokyo to shop for supplies.

We received a letter from Roger's sister Winnie one day. She told us she had an Armenian friend, whose brother had been in the Korean War and had met and fell in love with a lovely Korean woman. Winnie said he had some work to do in Tokyo and wondered if we had some room for him to sleep and eat. It would be just a few weeks, she said. So Roger wrote and told her the young man could come and stay with us, but he would have to use a taxi from the train station to our home. We would have a bed and meals for him.

When the young man arrived, he told us that meals would have to be on time when he got up and came home. We found him to be a very demanding young man. The weeks turned into months.

One evening, he returned home for his dinner and was met by our coworker Tahara san at the door. "Sir," Tahara san said, "you refuse to listen to sensei talk to you about Jesus, you demand they wait on you all the time, and you pay nothing to stay here. They have given you the best part of their small house, and now I have found you a room near the train station, and the lady is waiting for you now to feed you. We have wondered why you have been in Japan for so long now instead of going to pick up your girlfriend in Korea.

"Sensei did not ask me to do this," he continued. "I have watched you take advantage of them and took it upon myself to find a place, so do not blame them."

With that, they walked out with baggage and all and he never did say thank you.

Several days later, we received a report. The lady told Tahara san that the young man left for Korea a day later. Months later, we found out the girl had tuberculosis, and the American government had not cleared her to leave for the US. I'm not sure if he married her or even if he stayed in Korea or just what happened. It was out of our hands. Funny things happen when you are young missionaries in a new country. Some things we learned the hard way.

CHAPTER 21

Boarding School? Not My Daughter

Do not let your hearts be troubled; believe in God, believe also in Me.

—John 14:1

L iving in a different area of the world brought many challenges to which we adapted and learned to enjoy. Our third summer in Japan in 1953 brought more challenges. Linda had been attending kindergarten at the airbase and was thrilled with it. Her teacher arrived at my door one Saturday to see if I had any college education. "Several years but had not graduated," I told her.

"Meg," she said, "I need help. Would you be willing to teach Linda's class? I found that I am pregnant, and my doctor here says I must go back to America so I must find a teacher, and I thought about you."

Roger and I sat and talked about it. The cost associated with Linda's schooling would be cared for, and that was a nice plus. I'd love the teaching experience. Roger suggested that I go for it.

Linda's teacher told me she would work with me for a couple of weeks and show me how to lay out lesson plans. I was so excited. I had a Japanese ambassador's daughter in my class who was Linda's age. Working through kindergarten material was great, and Linda was home with us every day.

I enjoyed teaching Linda's kindergarten class. The Japanese ambassador's daughter was slow in learning English, and Linda was delighted to help her. Graduation day came. Sunflowers made of paper were placed around the faces of each child.

The ambassador's daughter came to me after our program said, "Mrs. Fox, thank you very much for teaching me English," and hugged me.

Tears filled my eyes. I had given her a start, and the first-grade teacher moved her along to learning more. It also was wonderful to see her in Sunday school from time to time.

It didn't end there. The principal of the base school asked me to continue teaching the class for another year. Linda could go to first grade, and they would pay for it. It took thirty minutes for Linda and me to walk to the train. That was twice each day.

I was going to teach kindergarten again when Linda was going to start second grade, and Roger had taken the responsibility to take her on the train and picking her up again. We were going through some very trying times in making decisions.

The Japan Bible Institute had closed for lack of students, but instead, a group of missions decided a K–12 school was necessary to teach their children. FEGC offered the Higashikurume property, and the Christian Academy in Japan (CAJ) was born. One day, the headmaster at CAJ came for a visit.

Virgil and Jeanette Newbrander were dear friends, and we were thrilled that they had taken the time to come visit. We had a great time catching up on things they were doing and things we were doing. Virgil asked the question, "When are you going to send Linda to boarding school at CAJ?"

I couldn't answer that question. "Boarding school?" I said. "No, Virgil."

She was our responsibility to teach. It was an awful day. We had lunch, and they went their way and said they would be praying for the decisions we faced. It was the worst day for me since we had been in Japan. However, God was in control.

Several days later, Roger had been to Yokohama on business and said he had signed us up to go to Lake Yamanaka for our first vacation in Japan. At the base of Mount Fuji, Japan's tallest mountain, there are five lakes. *Yamanaka-ko*, or Lake Yamanaka, is one of those five lakes. The mission had purchased the property with seven rustic cabins as a conference center or missionary retreat location when it became available in 1949.

We had a cabin with six other FEGC families for several weeks, but I had told Roger that I didn't want to go. What would we do about our Japanese classes? Sunday school? Teaching at the base? Who would stay in our home? We had to have a watchman.

But God!

I wrestled all summer about boarding school. I was miserable. Roger prayed with me and for me. We talked and talked, and one day he said, "Honey, why are we in Japan?"

I thought about that for a minute and said, "To reach the Japanese people in Hachioji for Jesus."

"Well, are we doing that?"

"Well, we have Japanese coming each night for Bible study."

Tahara san, Reto san, Muraoka san, Sato san, Koji san, Cheko san, Sakura san, Micheko san had all come to Jesus in those early years. Lots of kids had come to Jesus. At Tachikawa Air Base, young fellows had accepted Jesus.

"All good, but why are we here?"

"To start a church that will be a lighthouse for Jesus in this city," I said.

I started to cry. Language study had taken a back seat. I thought of all the things we were not doing to start a church. College young people and high school scholars were plentiful, and few parents cared. Most were steeped in Buddhism. They didn't care about God. It was an awful time in my life. It was the reason Linda wasn't going to boarding school. I wasn't even willing to find out if she would like it. We just never talked about it. I spent a lot of time on my knees in prayer that summer at Lake Yamanaka. Linda was having a wonderful time with Bonnie Newbrander and Cherry and Leroy Seibert.

I finally said, "Honey, I'm wrong. Just like God took care of Linda when she had virus X in South Carolina and took care of her in surgery to remove the walnut-sized tumor in her leg and took care of her when she had pneumonia, I know He will take care of her at CAJ."

As we snuggled in bed that night, Roger prayed, and peace filled my heart. I fell asleep with joy determined to see Virgil the next morning.

Dawn was beautiful. I looked out the cabin window and saw Virgil fanning the charcoal in the *hibachi* across the way. I got dressed and went out while it was still quiet and went to talk to Virgil. He greeted me cheerfully. He knew I had been hurting when they saw me last. "You have peace," he said. "What are you going to do?"

I rehearsed the events the night before and joy flooded my heart when I said yes to the Lord. Linda could go to boarding school.

"Have you told Linda?" Virgil asked.

I said, "We never even talked to Linda about it, but we will this morning."

I turned back toward our cabin and saw Roger fanning our *hibachi* and was cooking pancakes. Linda and Tim both were helping Dad, and Virgil was as happy as I was.

As I walked back to our cabin, Roger said, "You had victory."

"Yes," I said.

As we sat eating breakfast, Roger said he had something important to talk about, and the whole family listened.

"Boarding school?" Linda asked. "Oh, Daddy, that's wonderful. I can see Bonnie and Cherry every day. Oh, thank you, Mommy and Daddy."

She finished eating before running to tell her friends the news. It was a wonderful sunny day.

Uncle Virgil and Aunt Jeanette were down at the beach at the lake by the time we finished breakfast and cleaning up. Linda exploded with joy when she saw Virgil, and they talked about going to boarding school in the fall just a few weeks away. Jeanette had been giving swimming lessons to any of the children who wanted to learn, and our two loved that. It was as if the clouds were gone, and it was a great summer. Several days later, the jeep was packed, and we bumped our way over the mountain roads to Hachioji.

We had several weeks to get Linda ready for school. She was excited, as we were. Roger and I had some rearranging to do with our schedules. We took the children on the train and bus the first time to CAJ. It was a good hour trip each way. We found Linda's room, and she was excited. I could hear Virgil say, "It will be harder on you than it will be on Linda."

As we walked to the bus stop on the way back to Hachioji, we were shedding a lot of tears. However, God was healing our hearts.

Tim was feeling it the most because he was not going to have his sister around. I knew kindergarten was going to keep us both busy. As a project, we created a farm out of cardboard including a barn, silo, farmhouse, a pigsty, and a garage—all very detailed too. Making a tractor and other things to go with the farm was fun too, as was making a city with a church and school. We saved every piece of cardboard that we could find.

Yes, it was lonely without our little chatterbox, and we wondered and prayed all week for her. We were excited about picking her up and wondered if she missed us too. We soon found out as we pulled into the CAJ parking area. We caught a glimpse of her playing with some friends, and when she saw us, she called out, "Mom and Dad," and dashed off with her friends until we were ready to leave. It had been a good week for her, and as the days passed, we knew it had been the best decision for her. We knew the Lord would always care for her.

In fact, we learned many good lessons from the experience that continued to be blessings to us. One weekend, we had gone to pick her up at school, and her dorm mother said that Linda needed a raincoat, umbrella, and boots, and Linda said she had wanted a new skirt. We told her that she would have to wait about six weeks, for we had to write our parents and ask them for those things as there was no place in Hachioji to buy them for her.

Linda looked at us with a puzzled look on her face. "Can't we ask the Lord for them?" she asked.

We said sure, and we prayed right then. Only the Lord knew what lay ahead for us.

We waited a bit for her to gather her things and piled into the jeep for the trip back to Hachioji. The chattering between Linda and Tim was really special. She filled him in on CAJ, and he filled her in on kindergarten. Roger leaned over, took my hand, and squeezed it three times—our code for "I love you."

We had a busy weekend to get through before she went back to school Monday. Sunday morning, when we arrived home from church, there was a box sitting in the entryway of the house. It was from New Jersey and had been on the way for six weeks. It was addressed to Linda Fox.

What can I say? In the box was a raincoat and boots and an umbrella and a new skirt—all that fit her to a tee. We were so amazed. She smiled and said, "We prayed to the Lord for these things." A happy second grader went back to school after that weekend.

Our faith was small, but through the years in Japan, it grew and kept growing more and more as each year passed. Linda, Tim, and I played games in the street with the Japanese neighbor children whenever it was possible, and that was a joy, for we got to know them pretty well. I often would take a baby off a brother or sister's back, allow them to be free for a few minutes to jump rope, or I would hold one end of the rope to allow more to play.

One day, while we were playing, one of the kids asked me, "Why are you in our country, and why do you play with us?"

"You help me learn Japanese," I said, "and we are here to tell you about the Lord Jesus."

One said, "Tell us about Lord Jesus."

"In America," I said, "we have Sunday schools for children to come to, and they learn Bible songs and stories."

This seemed to interest them, and so I said, "Would you like to come to our house this Sunday and have a time to hear some Bible stories?"

They quickly responded, "Yes."

"What time is best for you?" I asked.

"Not morning but evening after dinner, and their parents were home," they said.

It was a very exciting time for us to think we were at last going to reach our neighbors for the Lord. Tahara san had prepared a lesson, and Kato san was clued into some songs. We were ready for them when they arrived at 8:00 p.m. that Sunday.

The two teachers were as shocked as we were when instead of seven or eight children showing up, we had fifty-eight children fill up the house. From where did they come? Apparently, the seven we initially invited told others. The American house was a real curiosity to them. They looked everywhere in the house, and then Tahara san got them organized and seated on the floor. It was exciting to hear them recite verses and to sing. From that first Sunday school class, six others were started in all parts of the city. Even the priest at a Buddhist temple told us we could use the temple yard for one of the Sunday school classes. We trained teachers on Saturday and then went out to teach on Sunday.

Linda, being a five-day boarder, had some downsides. Roger had secured a Harley-Davidson 250. It was small but good for Roger to come and go to CAJ with Linda. One weekend, when Linda was home, she asked at the dinner table, "Why do I come home on weekends? You are so busy. I get home Friday, and we rush through dinner. We play a bit, and then we're rushed off to bed so the Japanese young people can have Bible study.

"Saturday, Mom has a teacher's training class for the young Christians to learn how to teach Sunday school. Saturday afternoon, Dad has a preacher boy class so they can go out and share Jesus on the street and at the *eki* (train station).

"Sunday, it's off to base for Sunday school and church, home for dinner, and then pack me up for school, and off we go to CAJ.

"Why do I come home? I hardly see you. Boarding school is pretty good."

We were in a bit of shock to hear Linda talk like that, but she was right. We were busy and had little time for the kids on the weekend. We talked about it as a family, and all agreed something had to be done. But what? We were building God's church, and that was why we were in Japan.

Church planting was hard work. Was it going to come forth bearing fruit? Roger had been teaching a high school Bible class in the area of Kunitachi, which was about thirty minutes by train to the school where the boys met. It turned out that most of the boys lived closer to us than Kunitachi. Buildings were few and far between in Hachioji because of the damage done during the war. We could see progress in starting the church, so we moved the Kunitachi class to our home.

We both loved the Bible classes after school was out for the boys. No one worried or complained that we did not have any heat in the house. They loved coming to the house because they said our love was warm and didn't really care to go home at night. They did go home each night, but it usually was late.

We had Bible study classes each evening. Sometimes the lessons were from Genesis, other times from Mark and John. They knew little to nothing about Jesus and God and the Holy Spirit or the Bible. Each one brought their own Bible, and if anyone came to their first meeting without a Bible, they had one when they came back. The Pocket Testament League portable organ we brought with us from the states was well used in the classes, and we loved to hear those young people sing.

"What a Friend We Have in Jesus"

My friend Jesus is full of kindness and love.
Itsukushimi fukaki, Tomo naru Iesu wa
He took away my sins, my transgressions and my sadness.
Tsumi toga urei wo, Torisari tamou
I gave Him all of my grief and pain.
Kokoro no nageki wo, Tsutsumazu nobete
He took all of my burdens away.
Nadoka wa orosanu, Oeru omoni wo

My friend Jesus is full of kindness and love.
Itsukushimi fukaki, Tomo naru Iesu wa
He knows our weaknesses and shows compassion.

Warera no yowaki wo, Shirite awaremu
When I'm worried and sad and feeling down,
Nayami kanashimi ni, Shizumeru toki mo
He answers my prayers and comforts me.
Inori ni kotaete, Nagusame tamawan.

My friend Jesus is full of kindness and love.
Itsukushimi fukaki, Tomo naru Iesu wa
He leads me with unchanging love.
Kawaranu ai mote, Michibiki tamou
Though my friends in this world might leave me
Yo no tomo warera wo, sutesaru toki mo
He answers my prayers and cares for me.
Inori ni kotaete, Itawari tamawan.

"When I Survey"

When I look up at the Lord Jesus on the Cross,
Ju-jika ni kakarishi, Shu Iesu wo aogeba,
Wealth and fame are the same as trash.
Takara mo homare mo, Akuta to kawarazu

I cannot boast in anything but the Cross.
Ju-jika no hoka ni wa, Hokori no aranu mi,
Anything else will not move my heart.
Ikanaru mono ni mo, Kokoro wa ukokaji

The crown of thorns shines on His head
Mikashira ibara no, Kamuri ni kagayaki
From His hands and feet, sadness and grace bow.
On te ashi urei to, Megumi wo nagashitsu
In response to this grace, all I can do is offer my
body and soul to Him.
Megumi ni mukuyuru, Subenaki kono mi wa
I can do nothing but bow before Him.
Mi to tama sasagete, Nukazuku hoka nashi

This was the beginning of the church in Hachioji, and things were starting to fall into place. We had a wonderful group of young men and women coming. Presenting the good news of the gospel was so exciting, and telling of the birth of Jesus and about His life was the reason we were there. Teaching the highlights of what God's Word was about was a joy. Some nights, we fell into bed exhausted, wondering if they really understood our Japanese as we shared the Word of God.

To have someone say, "I want Jesus in my heart, sensei," always was a joy as we explained:

- *"For God so loved the world, that He gave His only begotten Son, that whoever believes in Him shall not perish, but have eternal life" (John 3:16).*

- *"For all have sinned and fall short of the glory of God" (Romans 3:23).*

- *"For the wages of sin is death, but the free gift of God is eternal life in Christ Jesus our Lord" (Romans 6:23).*

- *"But if we walk in the light, as He Himself is in the Light, we have fellowship with one another, and the blood of Jesus His Son cleanses us from all sin" (1 John 1:7).*

- *"If we confess our sins, He is faithful and just to forgive us our sins and to cleanse us from all unrighteousness" (1 John 1:9).*

- *"Come now and let us reason together, says the Lord. Though your sins are scarlet, they will be white as snow; though they are red as crimson, they will be like wool" (Isaiah 3:18).*

- *"But grow in the grace and knowledge of our Lord and Saviour Jesus Christ. To Him be the glory, both now and to the day of eternity" (2 Peter 3:18).*

- *"And then God's promise of a new heaven and a new earth, in that present creation will be destroyed so that it may be cleansed from all the effects of sin," as described in Revelation 21–22.*

It took months to get the message across because our dictionary English was slow. The Japanese language was so difficult; sometimes I thought I would never learn it.

During our time in Hachioji, we asked the Pocket Testament League to come and have a week of evangelistic meetings. We ended that week with 108 decision cards on which to follow up. Upon visiting, we found that not one really wanted to hear any more about the Lord, and thanked us for coming, and it ended there. Another time, we had a couple from Washington State come for special meetings. He played a musical saw, and she played a harp beautifully. Again, many cards were filled out and signed, and many said they wanted to hear more, but when we followed up, they were not interested at all.

It was most discouraging, but that was life in those seed-planting times. It was seed planting, to be sure. There was a harvest of fruit too when we saw so many of the college young people and high school–age students come to Christ. That work grew, and they really were a blessing to our hearts.

We learned too that you cannot start a church with just young people and expect it to be supported. High school–age kids finish their education and then move to another area to start college. Recent college grads finish their studies and move on to start their new careers.

CHAPTER 22

Trusting God for...Well, Everything

Trust in the Lord with all your heart
And do not lean on your own understanding.
In all your ways acknowledge Him,
And He will make your paths straight.

—Proverbs 3:5–6

When Roger and I were married, we knew our lives would be filled with trusting the Lord Jesus for every need. We chose without hesitation to go to the mission field, trusting the Lord for everything the family would need. We knew it was not going to be easy. We did not want people thinking that we were to be "charity" cases. We longed for the Lord to shine in and through us. Both our families initially thought going with a faith mission was not the thing to do. We are grateful my folks stood with us.

When Dad was up in years, he shared with us things about their lives that I did not know. During the Great Depression, he said they lost everything—home, back account, job, everything. He learned through word of mouth of two men who had started a business in Baltimore. Dad and Mom lived in Canton, Ohio, at the time. These two men were looking to hire another salesperson. It was decided that Dad would go and see what it was all about, so he took a bus, leaving Mother, my brother, and me, and went to Baltimore. They didn't know how long he would be away.

Baltimore was different than Canton. There were row homes everywhere, and their white steps were polished each morning and were immaculate. The two businessmen had a place for Dad in one of those row houses.

He recalled one evening he arrived at home after a long day at the office, walked in, and headed up the stairs to bed. But something didn't seem right. He had forgotten to hang up his coat on the rack downstairs, so he went back downstairs, but there was no rack. There was no one around, so he went back outside to see if he was in the right house. He quickly discovered that he was two doors away from his home. He carefully closed the door and went to his place, where he found everything, coat rack and all. No one locked front doors in those days.

The two men, who were professing Christians, decided that Dad was a good one to help in getting Business Equipment off the ground, so the family moved to be with him in 1931. Dad continued with these two men until one of the men proved to be a poor businessman and quit.

Dad, however, saw some potential in the business and bought their shares of the business and was on his own. He hired a man to make repairs on typewriters, adding machines, calculators, etc. He was a good man, but he was an alcoholic. When he was sober, he did a great job for my dad, but when he was drunk, he was not so good. Dad saw good in him and kept him on.

Dad needed some funds, he said, to really get the business going. Money was tight after the Depression, but one evening, at an elder's meeting at church, one of the men quietly asked Dad if he needed some money.

Dad said he had no idea how this man knew of his need, but Dad said he was interested but didn't want to borrow money from the bank. The man loaned him five hundred dollars—a lot of money at that time—and Dad promised to pay him back within six months. Dad paid the man back with interest within six months as promised. He said that was his first lesson in faith but not the last.

Also during that time, Mother was diagnosed with iritis and was told that she would never see again, but after many months and a neighbor's coming over to watch us kids each day, mother's sight returned. Another time, Dad ended up with bronchial pneumonia and was critical for some time and months later was healed. At that same time, I had blood poisoning from a cat scratch, my brother had to have both ears lanced. It was a troubling time in our lives.

Dad went on, but it was at that time that Dad decided to get into church and seek God's will for our lives. John Hess Macomb was pastoring a church within walking distance, and on a Sunday morning, Dad took my brother and me to Sunday school and church, leaving Mother home with our baby sister.

My dad was exhilarated after church, proclaiming, "Mother, we're going to church as a family next week. Baby will be fine."

From then on, we rarely missed Sunday school and church. My parents grew in the Lord and, one day, rededicated their lives to Jesus. Our home changed.

Dad and Mother had one vice in the world. Playing Bridge was a big part of their lives. We would not have a babysitter; we would get packed up and taken to the home of whoever was hosting Bridge that week. There were other kids to play with, and at 8:00 p.m., we were tucked into our blankets for bed and slept several hours while our parents continued to play.

When my folks turned their lives over to Christ, all of our lives changed. Playing Bridge became a thing of the past. *Eternity* magazine came to our house, and on the back page were lists of Bible verses we had to memorize. My dad became very active in Pocket Testament League and was president of the Baltimore chapter for many years. Child Evangelism Fellowship was just getting started when my parents rededicated their lives to the Lord. Mother would gather the children for classes for many years. Many accepted Jesus.

These were precious times in our home. She taught Sunday school to preschool-age children in our church for forty years and played the piano, had a craft each week, and guided the children in Bible memory work.

Pretty soon, our home became a haven for missionaries. It seemed like we entertained missionaries all the time. A bachelor was with us for dinner on most Sundays for years. Some Sundays, it was our bachelor friend and a widow and her two sons each week, and sometimes it would be fellows from the Princeton Choir that had sung in church that week. At other times, it was servicemen that had come to church, and we would have a couple each Sunday.

Mother often said they wondered where the food came from, but God always had enough on the table. Dad said over and over when he didn't know how they'd feed those folks, he would sell a typewriter and calculator. He and Mother were full of praise to God for caring for each of their needs. I found early in my life that missions were a priority in my home. Giving to the Lord's work also was a priority.

When Roger told me years later while we were dating, "I can't give you much, but by faith, we will trust Jesus for our needs," there were many times I said, "God, do just that."

There were several good examples. When our car broke down while we were in college, and the repair money—to the penny—arrived unexpectedly. Roger lost his paper route that we used to put food on the table. We were not just "pounded" by the wonderful people at High Hills Baptist Church in Horatio, but we were given more varied food than we had ever had—steak, pork chops, hamburger, potatoes, cereal, vegetables. Linda's X virus and walnut-sized tumor on her leg brought fear and concerns, but God showed us the right doctor who would take care of her.

When the Billy Graham Crusade was coming to Columbia, we wrestled with joining the counseling team, but we did. Counselors stood in the back each night of the packed house, but we would hear the message and the music. The best part, though, was that every evening, someone from our church in Horatio came to the back and either accepted Christ as their Savior or rededicated their lives to the Lord. We knew we would have a new congregation. It was a most rewarding week, and we did have a new church family with whom to share God's work. Our hearts were full of praise, and it was a good experience for our future church planting work in Japan.

How was a family of four going to travel across the country on our way to Japan with just fifty dollars in our pocket? That church in Florida stuffed Roger's pockets with cash and a gas credit card to provide the money we needed to get across the country.

Our lesson in faith grew as we saw God provide for us to go to Japan. By faith, God got us through Japanese language study. By faith, Ted found us the house in Hachioji. God had a wonderful purpose for our lives. We just had to walk a day at a time to see all this happen.

CHAPTER 23

Send Missionaries—Bibles
Are What They Need

He said to them, "Go into all the world and
preach the gospel to all creation. He who has
believed and been baptized shall be saved, but he
who has disbelieved shall be condemned."

—Mark 16:15–16

General Douglas McArthur had pleaded at the end of World
War II, "Send missionaries to Japan, not guns but Bibles are
what they need." Missionaries responded to McArthur's plea.
Getting the necessary education was first, and getting to Japan was
challenging, but we were there. Learning the language was difficult for
some, easier for others. Reaching the Japanese was a major challenge.
We had classes in college that taught us how to establish churches, but
we did not have classes on reaching a non-English-speaking population of a different culture.

Many of us new to Japan tried many things to reach the Japanese
for Christ, often with mixed results. We learned early during our time
in Hachioji that many high school and college-aged young people made
decisions for Christ. That was wonderful, but the age group was rather
transient. They would graduate from school then move somewhere else

where their career lead them. They were not the ones who would be helping to establish and maintain churches with a national pastor.

We prayed for God's direction to find ways to reach the people for Christ. We were willing to try just about anything. One method that worked for a while was to hold tent meetings in areas where there were small towns and small populations. Our friends and coworkers Rollie Reasoner and Shelton Allen had started an outreach program with several Japanese believers to start street preaching. They moved the street meetings to a large tent and found success reaching the people in the towns where they traveled.

The field chairman asked Roger to join the group as business manager, and they held many tent meetings over the next few years. Tents were portable, and people were used to them, so it was a good way to help the people come to know the Lord. It was a new experience for all, and it turned out to be one of the most wonderful ways to unite us missionaries that had become necessary after we all were moved to our different working areas.

Some of the single women missionaries were cooks for the team, some played instruments, and some, along with our Japanese coworkers, did visitation in the area and invited the families to come to the tent meetings. Flyers were put up everywhere and tacked to all poles available. Oh, yes, permission had to be obtained before anything could be done. That was a problem in some areas, but others were completely open to whatever the foreigners wanted to do. It was a wonderful way to get the church off the ground in the areas where the tent was being set up.

Today, churches that had missionaries to follow up in the areas where tent meetings were held still are going strong. Where there was nothing, there now are more than fifty churches, and for that, we really praised the Lord.

Along with Roger's work on the tent team, he also was on the FEGC field council and the CAJ school board. He actively helped start two servicemen centers.

The tent work continued on into our second term, but it had a waiting period while Roger went back to language school after our first furlough, and I had a private teacher to tutor me. In less than two years, Roger was ready to hit the road with the tent team, and after rounding up some young people who were zealous to reach their own people, they were off with the blessing of the mission leadership.

Up in the mountains and through ridges of mountains, the team traveled and many came to know the Lord. One of the team, Fukuda san, was a wonderful personal worker and had a great heart for the elderly. He was out in one village, and an old woman came to the door and said she had been praying to the true God for years. When he told her about God, she responded, "I have been looking for years for someone to come and tell me about the person who made me and this whole earth."

His heart was really touched as he talked to her about the Lord. Then she said, "I want that God in my heart."

Tears poured that day in two people's hearts as the seed was there from the Lord, and Fukuda san saw her through for the Lord. She was too old to attend the tent meetings, but he visited her from time to time as he was in the area. Much seed was planted through the tent meetings.

While tent meetings did not produce indigenous churches, they did produce *dendojos* (meeting places). After a few years, even the *dendojos* closed unless a missionary stuck to the goals of seeing a church established. Some of the baby work died on the vine. As the story of the sower and the seed in Matthew, where there was a full-time missionary, a church was established and is indigenous today.

While the tent meetings were going strong, I was home with our children. With two in school and one at home and my language studies each day, it was a busy life, one that I look back on with joys as well as sorrow.

The kids and I loved our weekends together and being a family when Roger would come down from the mountains. I didn't like the loneliness of the life I lived, though. I became discouraged and frustrated and studied so hard to get the language, and I was succeeding, but the Lord took me to Deuteronomy and the wandering of the Israelites in the desert for forty years to teach me that I could take care of my loneliness and frustrations by trusting Him more. I loved those times in the Word, and I soon realized that He was with me all the time.

CHAPTER 24

Higashikurume

And now I commend you to the word of His grace, which is able to build you up and to give you the inheritance among all those who are sanctified.

—Acts 20:32

After we returned from furlough in 1957, we lived in Higashikurume, in a small house on a knoll about a five-minute walk for Linda and Tim to attend CAJ. Gary still was a toddler at the time. We had felt it was better for the family if we settled in a home near school, and Roger would travel with the tent team since it was not stationary work. And it worked out well. The house did not have any heat source when we moved in, so Roger and a few workers dug out under the house to make room for a furnace. He also installed all the duct work, and we had heat. That was not the first or only furnace Roger installed for people.

Roger never gave up his love for flying. He often would rent or borrow a plane just to get back up in the air. Once, a missionary in Kofu, west of Tokyo, bought a rug in Tokyo but wasn't sure how to get it to their location in Kofu. Roger and our friend Bill Viekman borrowed a single-engine, four-seater plane, stuffed the carpet inside, and flew it to Kofu. There wasn't any place to land, so they buzzed the missionary, and when they came outside, they dropped the carpet out of the plane in a field near their house. Delivery accomplished.

A couple of years later, the Kunigoshi family built a house next to us. In time, Mrs. Kunigoshi asked me to teach her English, and I said yes. We worked out a nice arrangement. I taught her English, and she would babysit Gary when we needed. Gary was like a sponge and learned to speak fluent Japanese from this family. We studied together for three years each Thursday night. Each time I would try to talk to her about Jesus, she would change the subject. However, one night, she didn't understand the difference between "feet" and "feat," and I had the joy of telling her about Yoneko san's testimony. Before she left that night, she asked Jesus into her heart. The next week, our English class was more Bible study than English.

It was about that time that the Lord gave me a great burden to reach women for the Lord. The more I studied, the more I had to give out, and the more I wanted to have some women with whom to share. God had a better plan, and I am glad He helped me through the language books and gave me time to study His Word. It was a wonderful time for all of us.

By the end of our second term, though, things in Japan were changing, and how we reached the Japanese changed with the coming of television. People didn't want to come out at night to the tent meetings because they didn't want to miss one of their new favorite television programs.

Our desire from the beginning of our ministry was to see the church established in Japan. We learned from our first term that you couldn't start a church with only young people because they were transient. They were not the ones who would be sustaining a national church.

Too many times, we had to move our church services in Hachioji, and each of these moves meant losing some people. We found that baptism separated families because we could not get with the family to explain why their son or daughter wanted to be baptized. Instead of seeing a family united in the Lord, we were tearing families apart.

We found that the old denominational churches in the country had taught that baptism was a graduation service instead of a matriculation time of going on with the Lord. That caused some problems. Young people out of Buddhist homes were the biggest problems. Parents were very unhappy when they heard that their children had accepted the Christian way.

So we learned many things those early years. When you are starting from scratch, you do learn as you go, and making mistakes is part of the learning process. Correcting them in time is next. It took three terms over the years to see the church in Hachioji be on its own with its own pastor and supported by the people of the church. We praise the Lord that it is free today and going well.

With tent meetings a thing of the past and our second furlough behind us, we returned to Japan in 1962, looking forward to starting a church in an area where there was no church, with the right goals in mind and with much prayer behind us from prayer warriors stateside.

The children were excited to be back in Japan. Linda was a sophomore in high school, Tim was in junior high, and Gary was in third grade. Friends made room for Roger and me to stay near CAJ, and the kids all were placed in dorms.

The field council told us about three areas they wanted us to pray about and to consider. The council was right there with us in all the decision-making and prayer, and we counted on the council for the final decision. It was wonderful to see how the Lord opened doors.

One of the three areas we were asked to consider was a *danchi* (a community of high-rise apartment buildings) that usually had about thirteen thousand to twenty-five thousand people living in them. People living in these apartments stayed until they saved enough money to move closer to the husband's place of employment. They didn't know how long they would be living in the area. Most missionaries didn't like working in a *danchi* because people were always moving on. We knew too that men were hard to reach because of their work schedule and travel time to and from those jobs, but there were a lot of women who were receptive.

We liked it because it reminded us of the dispersion and the way they went from Jesus to tell others about Him. It exercised our faith too to see these people come to the Lord. It wasn't an easy place to work, but it was good, and we really looked forward to the work.

We were introduced to two men from New Life League, a mission group that ran a printing facility and had a burden to reach the people living in the Higashikurume *danchi* near them. Arnfinn Andaas and Fred Jarvis took us to the *danchi* in an area we had not seen before, and it was only twenty minutes away from CAJ. That meant the kids could commute and didn't need to live in the dorms.

The *danchi* was about a year old. All of the apartments were occupied, we learned, with white-collar workers who worked in government, business, or for the air traffic control center. We wondered if we would fit in to the area with all these highly educated people, but we knew we had something they didn't have with all of their education—faith in the Lord Jesus.

When we toured the area, we found row after row of four- and five-story apartment buildings. It was situated on former farmland and was so new, stores and other businesses still were being built and certainly no home for us to rent, and that became our biggest challenge.

Park and Jan Rohrer, a couple who lived near Fuchu Airbase about forty-five minutes away, were building a house on the New Life League compound. They offered us the house they were living in when their new house was complete. We looked at it and found it was suitable to our needs and was still a reasonable bus ride for the children to get to school.

When we went to sign the lease with the family, Park said, "This is ridiculous. We would live there and work here, and you would live here and work there. You need to live there and work in the *danchi*. The Lord would not be pleased with this arrangement."

So we moved into their new not-quite-finished home, which was five minutes from the *danchi* and twenty minutes to CAJ, and completed the final projects to make it ready for living. Our former house worker from our second term, Furuyama san, even came and helped us unpack our freight, bag, and baggage. That night, the house looked like it had never been empty. We knew we were in *danchi* ministry not by chance but by His appointment.

Unknown to us, Fred Jarvis had arranged for Bible study meetings in an office building on the New Life League compound. We attended the meetings, and a few people came each night that weekend. We also found there was a small Sunday school class for children that met in the printing press area. When those evening meetings were over, Fred was reminded that the Foxes were there to start a church in the *danchi*, and he graciously took a step back.

All the planning and organizing for *Katayama Fukuin Kyokai* (Katayama Gospel Church) from then on was up to us. We had a wonderful time laying out plans to reach the people. We had oodles of ideas, but all of them had to be researched. We found there were things that we could not do in the *danchi*. For example, we could not have a religious meeting in the *danchi*, but when Roger explained that we were looking for a place to have a musical program, they agreed, and the date was set.

We advertised to all we could. Our whole family, children and all, put flyers in all the mailboxes and let all know about the meeting in the *danchi* recreation room. We did not know who would come, but we had a good program. Tahara san was going to play a musical saw that he had learned, and a former missionary kid back in Japan with the military was going to play trumpet.

The program lasted more than an hour, and we gave out cards for information from all who came with a note, where they could sign if they were interested in hearing more about Jesus Christ. With these cards, we had names with whom to follow up. We found that some had come from other churches in other areas, and they were too far away to attend and were looking for a new church home.

It was Miyazaki san that first Sunday after the special meetings who said, "I will go with you to visit. I can tell you what to do and do it properly. You are younger than I, and so when we get to a home where the woman is older, I will talk to her. When it is a younger woman, you talk to her. We will pray for each other as the other talks."

That approach sounded familiar because that was what my roommate Anne and I did in our personal evangelism class at Columbia Bible College. Miyazaki san met me at the entrance to the *danchi*. We visited in as many homes as we could in three or four hours. It was rewarding to talk to each one who opened the door, and I felt very at ease with Miyazaki san there. We did that for several weeks.

In that time, we had some folks coming to church in the office who did not like the old rickety chairs on which we were sitting. They asked if they could make cushions for the chairs. The tasks were divided among the women, and they arrived at our home on Thursday to start class in *zabuton* (cushion) making. This is an art in Japan. We had such fun and my Japanese improved with each gathering.

After one *zabuton* session, one of the ladies asked, "This has been wonderful. Would you consider continuing these gatherings with a Bible class for us? We want you to teach us."

I thought of the lessons learned in our second term and the hours of studying the Word of the Lord, and here they were asking me to teach them. I told them they were welcome to come, but Asazaki san was much more able to teach them in their language.

They were stunned. "Sensei," they said, "we want you to teach us."

I argued inside, *I can't*, but God said, "You spent many years studying the language, you prayed for families to come to Christ, you were burdened to teach women, and I am now opening the door."

I couldn't argue with God, and so I agreed.

Seven women came the next week, then eight or nine. Next thing I knew, there were fifteen attending. My halted Japanese improved. But more than that, the women knew I loved them. I could see the women walking on the path coming through the woods to our house to study God's Word each week. Some were old in the Lord; some were seekers who knew nothing about God and His son Jesus or that they were sinners and needed the blood of Christ to cleanse them from all their sin.

Then one week, when we finished *fujinkai* (study group), Miyazaki san told me her family was moving to different location. She was the oldest in the Lord in our group. I really had come to love her. It was a real heartache to know that she and her family would no longer be coming. Who would go with me the following Tuesday?

No one, but God had something to teach me and that He still was there, and that was exciting.

I went that following Tuesday, reluctantly, really hoping that I would not have to talk to anyone about the Lord. That was quite a rebuke. I had lined up six to eight apartments to visit. It didn't really take long because no one was home. My faith was sure being stretched. I really had been afraid to go alone. I went because I knew it was an important part of the work for the Lord.

When I returned home so soon after I had left, Roger asked what had happened. When I told him what happened, he said, "Well, honey, go out again. There will be some people home next time."

I felt terrible. I didn't care if they were home or not. I didn't like going alone.

The second week, I had to pray myself into going again and went. This time, there were a few people at home and welcomed my visit. I even had tea with several, and I went home singing for joy and praising the Lord.

The next Sunday, another saint of the Lord with her two little ones volunteered to go with me. I enjoyed her fellowship, and we made some more good contacts. The woman's work was growing. Eventually, eight or nine women went into the *danchi* each week going to apartments and talking about Jesus.

At *fujinkai*, we started with the wordless book. That took about a year to get through. Step-by-step the women could see what sin was, why the blood of Jesus was shed, and how our hearts could be white as snow, that there was a period until we met the Lord in heaven. It meant repetition all the time for there were newcomers each week as our group grew in leaps and bounds.

I didn't have to prove the Bible in *fujinkai*. I wanted them to see their need for Jesus. Each loved the Bible; they loved to sing from the hymnbook, and each memorized a verse weekly. Little by little, they began to share the word with others.

CHAPTER 25

The Danchi Church Grows

And the Lord was adding to their number day by
day those who were being saved.

—Acts 2:47

The second year, we studied the Old Testament, hitting the highlights as we went—creation, Noah, Abraham, Joshua, David, Samuel, Ruth, Esther, prophecies of Jesus's coming. The next year was New Testament studies. The year after was applying the lessons to the heart, using toy animals (i.e., peacock for pride, mule for stubbornness, rooster as a braggart, sheep as a follower) to show how we each are different, but we are all sinful people. We have the need for Jesus in our lives.

Roger became more and more involved with the men from church. They had a meeting in the evening and shared about business and things about themselves. Roger followed with a Bible study. We started our first English night class, and that was a good way to make contacts. I taught English, and Roger taught the Bible after that. I also had a high school–age English class and then finished with a Bible lesson.

No one had to pay for the classes. If someone wanted to pay, I would say that pay was to be in church that Sunday morning. I was happy when they came. Roger was the Sunday school teacher and pastor of the church and the men's leader. English became our second language instead of our first. We spoke English with family, and that was about all. We were seeing so many people come and one by one accept the Lord.

We had been praying and searching for a Japanese coworker. Our prayers were answered. A man who had been working at the New Life League printing plant, Miyamoto san, had been attending a Christian seminary but was taking a year off. He and Roger met, and he started coming to church. The more he came, the more Roger felt he was God's choice for the work.

Miyamoto san left the press to work with us full-time, and he fit in well. The people enjoyed him, and he loved the work. He returned to seminary after the year was over and graduated two years later.

He had tuberculosis as a young man and had been in a sanitarium for quite a while, and it was there that he was led to Christ. He was not a fresh-out-of-seminary Christian worker; rather, he was a mature man with a love for the Lord and had a tremendous burden to see his people come to Christ.

He worked hard with Roger, laying out the plans for the year. He did have a few weaknesses, but who doesn't. One of his weaknesses was with me. Japanese have an obligation system called *giri*. In Japan, *giri* means "duty" or "debt of gratitude," or "social obligation." The most common way it comes out in daily life is when a gift is given or a favor is done for someone. The recipient of the gift or favor feels strongly obligated to make repayment. It can be almost as strong as a Westerner's feeling of need to repay a financial loan, so it is not uncommon for gifts to be given back and forth, sometimes seemingly with no end. Another way to observe *giri* is in daily business life through customer service. It is common to find a level of servitude and formality in employees at all levels of an organization.

When we began the work in the *danchi*, we encouraged people not to have obligation to us but to God. Miyamoto san had *giri* to me, and he thought he should have it. In time, things worked out as he learned the women in the church did not have *giri* to me, but it was to the Lord as it should be.

We knew that to continue the work in the *danchi*, Miyamoto san needed to find a wife, and we prayed toward that end. A Christian man we knew, Murase san, became Toyoshima san's *nakadachi* (intermediary) and suggested her to Miyamoto san. Miyamoto san went to meet with her, liked her, and after a while, proposed marriage. She accepted.

Then her pastor, Oyama san, squelched the relationship, partly because Murase san, his brother-in-law, had gone behind his back in arranging the marriage. Miyamoto san didn't want to make a problem, so he told her she should listen to her pastor and withdrew his proposal.

We found out later that Oyama san had told Toyoshima san relatively nothing about the work in the *danchi*, and apparently, Miyamoto san had not talked much about the work either. Oyama san also told her "any work that is carried out by the missionaries would go to pieces when the missionary leaves."

Betty Meyer, a friend of ours and a missionary with Hi-BA, called me one day on behalf of a friend of Toyoshima san to ask what we were doing in the *danchi*. After I told of the work we were doing, we agreed that we needed to help Toyoshima san understand. I invited her to come visit with me and to speak at *fujinkai*. She did, and I found her to be a terrific girl. We had a grand time together. She then knew that there was a need for a wife to work with the pastor in the church. She also spoke at a *fujinkai*, and the women in the group loved her.

Toyoshima san sent her pastor an angry letter about what he had done. He apologized to Miyamoto san, and they spent a Saturday talking about the work in the *danchi* and about his desire to have Toyoshima san as his wife. She came back several times before they were married, talking to the *fujinkai*, and we all liked her more and more each time.

Because of the success God provided, other missionaries began to look into *danchi* ministry and found it as rewarding as we did.

Our goal was families united in Christ, with an indigenous church led by a national pastor at the end of our five-year term. This was our prayer, and we saw God doing just that.

God blessed our ministry in the *danchi*, and I would love to tell about each and every man, woman, and child who made decisions for Christ, but that would fill volumes.

CHAPTER 26

The Tazaki Family

> Only conduct yourselves in the manner worthy
> of the gospel of Christ, so that whether I come
> and see you or remain absent, I will hear of you
> that you are standing firm in one spirit, with one
> mind striving together for the faith of the gospel.

> —Philippians 1:27

Katayama Gospel Church had its first musical program in the *danchi* in 1964, and as a result of that night of music, Mrs. Tazaki and her daughter Kiyoko chan came to the church. She had attended another church in southern Japan before moving to Higashikurume. She had prayed for many years for her husband to be saved. In March that year, he started attending the Saturday night English conversation class. He seemed to have a very open heart, and after several weeks, he began to attend church too. In May, he made a decision for the Lord.

One night, at choir practice, Mrs. Tazaki said, "My children have a new father. I have a new husband, but my husband has a new life."

Daughter Kiyoko chan accepted Jesus as her Savior in April that year. Mr. Tazaki was baptized in May, and Kiyoko chan followed in June. Mrs. Tazaki started teaching Sunday school that summer, and she said in class one day, it was a blessing to her to be able to have time to study the Bible when preparing for the class. And not even her job got in the way when it came to help in the work of the Lord.

Mr. Tazaki's mother lived with them. We found out that she had cancer and didn't have long to live. He was convinced his mother was happy not knowing about Jesus but then realized he needed to witness to her. She became senile and died in December that year. The funeral was Buddhist, and we were concerned. He was convinced that she should have the Buddhist funeral because she was Buddhist and had requested one.

Many people attended the funeral including several from church. We had a special prayer meeting for the Tazaki family. The funeral itself was a real testimony to the Lord's grace. Neither Tazaki san nor his family worshipped as Buddhists did by bowing to the dead, crying, or making sounds of sorrow. The Lord undertook in a marvelous way so the family had a positive witness for the Lord Jesus.

Mr. Tazaki was elected church treasurer in January the next year. He was very conscientious about the job. The family was very interested in the church getting organized. In February, we had our first *katei shukai* (home Bible study) at the Tazaki home. Because Mrs. Tazaki worked full-time selling pianos, it fell to Mr. Tazaki to clean their home before the meeting, which he did joyfully. When no one volunteered their home for the next *katei shukai*, Mr. Tazaki invited everyone to come back to their home the following week.

When she was free, Mrs. Tazaki went with me to visit ladies in the *danchi*. This family portrayed for the Lord all that is good about being a follower of Christ—zeal, joy, and love all wrapped into one.

CHAPTER 27

The Nakajima Family

No one has seen God at any time; if we love one another, God abides in us, and His love is perfected in us.

—1 John 4:12

At one of the *katei shukai* at the Tazaki home on a Saturday night, Roger took a movie on the life of Yoneko san and her attempt at suicide and showed it to two couples from the air control center. Mr. and Mrs. Nakajima both indicated that they were believers and had attended church elsewhere, but they had no happiness in their lives.

Mrs. Nakajima came to church the next day and said she would not leave until she knew how to accept the Lord. Little did we know then how much that family would come to mean to us. She went home that day radiant and became a faithful attendee of Sunday school, church, *fujinkai*, and choir. She became concerned for her husband because she came to believe that he never actually invited Jesus into his life, and she was really burdened for his salvation.

Roger spent an afternoon taking with him about the Lord. His heart was open, but he still didn't make a decision for Christ. He attended the Saturday English class and attended church fairly regularly but had to leave early because of his children. He was interested in attending Roger's Saturday study on John but didn't make it.

Mrs. Nakajima was baptized in May 1965. She became a dear friend and a valuable person in the church.

When someone was so close to accepting God's gift of salvation, it was not easy to keep working with an individual, except to leave it in God's hands. After all, God's timing is perfect.

CHAPTER 28

The Asazaki Family

You did not choose me, but I chose you and appointed you so that you might go and bear fruit, and that your fruit will remain, so that whatever you ask of the Father in My name He may give to you.

—John 15:16–17

One of the dearest, gentlest ladies I have ever met was Asazaki san. She had five wonderful children, three sons and two daughters. Toshiko san and Takao san came faithfully with her to church. Takao san studied a series of lessons with one of the Sunday school teachers. Mrs. Asazaki studied with him and gained a great deal from the study.

What a joy it was to be in their home over and over again to talk with them about Jesus Christ. She became a witness to her friends and neighbors. When she was a child, she had attended Sunday school near her home in Chiba Prefecture. She recalled little of that time. As a young girl, she thought that maybe she heard and accepted the plan of salvation, but it wasn't clear to her. Then one day in the *danchi*, she saw me walk by and how happy I was because I was smiling.

She told me later that she had asked herself, how could someone from America leave her family and friends and still be happy in this country? What makes her happy? Now she knows because she accepted Christ as her personal Savior. She told me she had been a Buddhist, but she was never healthy as a Buddhist but had been feeling so good since she accepted Christ. Her heart was so happy. She was so happy the day that Takao san was baptized.

In June that year, she fell ill with a high fever. She was in bed for two months and in her apartment without leaving for about five months. The ladies started a prayer meeting, praying fervently for her health. She was in church the next Sunday.

Her husband was not interested, but Mrs. Tazaki told me that Takao san had been witnessing to his father. He realized that since he had become a Christian, his life had changed.

Mrs. Asazaki loved our children and often invited them over to their home Sunday afternoon for snacks and fellowship. I think she really loved having our kids over so that she could spoil them, and that was fine with us.

Takao san and Tim became fast friends and have kept up that friendship to this day.

CHAPTER 29

Shimoyoshi San

Consider it all joy, my brethren, when you
encounter various trials, knowing that the testing
of your faith produces endurance.

—James 1:2–3

Shimoyoshi san became a dear friend to me. A Christian friend
brought her to *fujinkai* one December. Nakajima san and several others had been talking with Shimoyoshi san. She then
attended church. Roger and I visited with her at Christmas time,
and she told us she had planned on attending the Christmas party,
hoping to bring her husband, too. At the last minute, he cancelled,
but she attended and had a wonderful time.

I didn't see her for a couple of weeks, and then in January, Mrs.
Tazaki, Mrs. Nakajima, and I visited in her home, and she attended
fujinkai the next day. I gave the lesson on the heart, and she seemed
to be burdened, so I asked if she'd like to stay and talk, and she
did. Before she left that afternoon, she accepted the Lord into her
heart and prayed a simple prayer, confessing sin and rejoicing in her
new friend Jesus Christ. It was exciting to me. She left after telling
Roger of her decision to serve Jesus. From then on, she tried to be in
church, *fujinkai*, and prayer meeting each week. She even offered her
apartment for ladies English class each week.

She was genuinely happy but was having struggles with her husband because he had many drinking friends and wanted them over to their home on Sunday nights. When she asked her husband if she could be baptized, he said, "Absolutely not!"

When Shimoyoshi san first became a Christian, her mother-in-law moved into the home and would not let her have any Christian fellowship and ordered her to "return the foreigner's God."

She endured continuous pressure from both families to "divorce" her faith in Christ. For the next year or so, it seemed the only time we saw her was when her mother-in-law was not around. We met her on the street one time while her mother-in-law was staying with them. She told us that she was pregnant and asked us to pray for strength from the Lord and that each need may be met.

Her baby was born the day after her sister had been killed. It was a sad and happy time for her. Right after, she called Roger and me and asked us to come visit her, her mother, and another sister. We talked with them for two hours and had ample time to witness to a sad mother and sister. The mother said, "My daughter has peace, and I don't know why."

Over the next several years, she attended church and *fujinkai* when she could and told us that her husband still was giving her a hard time about the Lord. She said she had witnessed to him, but he shunned everything she was telling him. He still was standing firm against her being baptized.

Roger and I went to see him about her being baptized. He was very friendly, and we had a good visit. Their child started acting up, so we didn't get a chance to get more serious talking done, but it was the most profitable afternoon in the life of this young family. He asked many questions and really seemed open to the work. He still wasn't willing to allow his wife to be baptized, but he didn't come out and say absolutely not, as he had previously.

The next week, she was in church with their son, and then the next week, Mr. Shimoyoshi babysat so that she could go to church. Little by little, we saw God working in this family. A few weeks later, he was in a terrible auto accident going to work and was saved from death. She really gave praise to God, and he evidently saw that God had been watching over him.

Shimoyoshi san and her family moved away to near Narita Airport east of Tokyo. She had not had regular Bible study or fellowship with other Christians. Her maturing in the Lord came to a standstill.

In 1980, when Roger and I were back in Japan for a three-year term, we caught up with Shimoyoshi san. On October 25 that year, she cried in her bed and asked God to help her. That same night, Nakajima san, her sister in the Lord from the *danchi* church, awoke from a dream about Shimoyoshi san and prayed for her. The next morning, she called her long-lost friend and invited her to the Billy Graham Crusade. "Meet me at gate 7," Nakajima san told her. And she did.

Later, when the invitation was given, Shimoyoshi san went forward. Later, she returned to the stands where Roger and I were waiting, and with tears in her eyes, she said, "I have rededicated my life to the Lord."

Turning to me she said, "Sensei, please find me a church near my house."

A couple of weeks later, Nakajima san, Roger, and I met in her home. All of us, along with two friends she had invited, had a meal together, and then in the afternoon, we had a Bible study with her two children as well. After that, we went looking for the church we had researched for her. The pastor's wife answered the door when we knocked and told us her husband was away, but she invited us all in. We immediately discovered we had mutual friends and a warm spirit of love and fellowship in the Lord.

Shimoyoshi san's husband had wanted to come home early from work to see us but was delayed so he asked us to meet him halfway between home and his office for a meal. We met, and he was very warm and cordial, and he asked us to stay overnight or at least come again when we could spend the night in their home.

And her mother-in-law? That same woman said, "All these years I have given you a hard time, and yet you have always been kind and sweet to me. Can you give me a book that will tell me how to be like you?"

Shimoyoshi san handed her a Bible.

CHAPTER 30

The Kitahara Family

We also exult in our tribulations, knowing that
tribulation brings about perseverance; and perseverance, proven character and proven character,
hope; and hope does not disappoint, because the
love of God has been poured out within our hearts
through the Holy Spirit who was given to us.

—Romans 5:3–5

Our first contact with the Kitahara family was through the
English conversation classes we offered on Saturday night. Mr.
Kitahara told me that he was born in Formosa (now Taiwan)
to Japanese parents. He attended church several times with his wife.
Their daughter Ginko chan began to attend Sunday school and church.
Then they sort of tapered off in their church attendance. Mrs. Kitahara
attended *fujinkai* semiregularly, and Ginko chan was pretty good about
getting to Sunday school.

I had been encouraging Ginko chan to get her parents to church,
and the next Sunday, they did attend. At Christmas time, I found out
that Mrs. Kitahara had been saved and baptized when she was young. A
couple months later, she told Roger that her husband was home with a
bad heart. She started attending church more often as well as an English
class. Little by little, the wall was breaking down. She started to become
friendlier, which was evidence that the Lord was working in her life.

Several others in the church noticed the difference in her life as well. In one of our weekly Bible studies, she went into the kitchen and started to do all the dishes. That small act really touched me because none of the other ladies seemed concerned. She was more and more willing to come to church and to study God's Word. Mrs. Nakajima invited her to prayer meeting, and she was so happy to be invited. She was one of the eight ladies attending and also desired to see their husbands saved.

A couple of months later, Mr. and Mrs. Kitahara both had been attending church quite regularly. He seemed to have a tender heart for the things of the Lord, so we kept praying. In May that year, Mr. Kitahara traveled to Switzerland for his job, and he was gone for two months. We prayed for his safety and security for Mrs. Kitahara and Ginko chan. When he returned, she told me that she was comforted by Romans 5:3–8 while she was waiting for his return. She praised God for getting her through those days of loneliness.

For a couple of years, we had been hosting a Christmas dinner for people from the church. We cleared the furniture out of the living/dining room. Roger then took all the doors in the house off their hinges and used them to make tables. We covered them with table-cloths, added chairs, and we had a banquet hall in our home. It was tight sometimes, but we could squeeze forty to fifty people around the "tables," and everyone had a wonderful time.

Mrs. Kitahara took over the Christmas supper one year, and it was a thrill to see her take on the responsibilities that went along with the meal. She told me she had memory verses on large paper in her kitchen where she can learn the verses and where her husband had to see them too.

I found out a few months later that she was a trained Sunday school teacher. I was thrilled because this was an area in which we had need. With some coaching, she started teaching the little children and found the experience highly rewarding.

Mr. Kitahara started showing more interest, and he became more involved with the work but still had not made a decision for Christ. At the end of that year, the family moved to another location for his job. We missed them and kept praying for his salvation.

CHAPTER 31

Suga San

For this is the love of God, that we keep His commandments; and His commandments are not burdensome. For whatever is born of God overcomes the world; and this is the victory that has overcome the world—our faith.

—1 John 5:3–4

My first contact with Suga san was when Linda was teaching English to her daughters Toshoko chan and Sumiko chan. I knew that Mrs. Suga spoke English, but there was a film between us, and I couldn't get to her. She was very faithful in attending *fujinkai*, always friendly, but standoffish, too.

The other ladies in the *fujinkai* started praying for her salvation. The next January, I taught a heart lesson, and during this lesson several hearts were touched, including hers. At the end of the lesson, she said in very good English, "My husband is a devout Buddhist but does not want me to attend church. I must obey his wishes. However, I must talk to you sometime."

So later that month we visited. She welcomed me with open arms and handed me two yellow cards. On each was written the plan of salvation in English from the Sunshine Club in Bolivia signed by each of her girls. They had lived in Bolivia for a year and in Boston for about fifteen months. She had contact with churches in each of those locations. She had made a decision for Christ some thirteen years earlier and had been baptized. Soon after, she was married to a devout Buddhist in an arranged marriage. She had not gone to church since because he had requested that she not go to church, and she had obeyed.

He had known that she was not happy, and the day she heard the heart lesson, she went back home and told her husband and their daughters. He in turn told her that if she really wanted to go to church, she could go if it meant that much to her. She and her daughters attended Sunday school and church faithfully after that.

Roger and I visited with her and talked about the truth of the Bible, and by degrees, she started seeing the truth. She read her Bible and really grew in the Lord. At the first prayer meeting she attended, she praised the Lord for being able to be back in the fellowship of Christians and the Lord.

Several months later, Suga san told me that she and her daughters had been reading their Bibles and praying each night. Each night, the girls have been praying for their dad to come to church and be saved.

One of the girls asked her dad why he didn't go to church with them some Sunday. He said he liked to sleep then. The daughter told her mother that she started praying that God would keep him awake so that he would start attending church. But he didn't want to have anything to do with us and made no bones about it. That didn't stop his family from praying for his salvation.

CHAPTER 32

Miyazaki San and Fukuda San

For I am not ashamed of the gospel, for it is the power of God for salvation to everyone who believes, to the Jew first and also to the Greek.

—Romans 1:16

Miyazaki san had been attending the church in the *danchi* since the beginning. She originally was from Kyushu, an island in Southwestern Japan, and her parents and grandparents had been Methodists just about their entire lives. Her husband had attended church regularly too, just not the same church.

She was very faithful and eager to learn what God said in His Word. She was so happy to have Roger and me teach God's Word, and it was such a joy to her. She helped Nakajima san clean the church each week and worked with Roger on kindergarten plans. She helped wherever she could.

She wanted so much to have her husband make a decision for Christ, but after a while, he started keeping her from church, and the things of the Lord. Between her husband's discouragement and her children getting sick from the measles, chicken pox, and colds, she had been attending irregularly. When she did return to *fujinkai*, she said the group felt so new because there were so many new folks.

Her mother visited one week, and they came to church together, and her mother got after her to get busy for the Lord. She really scolded her for being so lax in her help for the Lord. Miyazaki san started teaching the kindergarten class, which was a big need. She continued to teach the children and also became a better witness to other women in the group, including Fukuda san.

At first glance, Miyazaki san and Fukuda san could be sisters. Fukuda san had such a sweet, open heart and had been helping Nakajima san and Miyazaki san clean the church each week. Miyazaki san asked her from time to time when she was going to accept the Lord, and Fukuda san always said, "Not yet."

A short time later, when the invitation was given, she immediately raised her hand, saying she wanted to accept the Lord into her heart. After class, I asked if I could come see her. She readily agreed. We met at her home over tea and cake, and we chatted for a while.

Finally, Fukuda san said she had a problem. She showed me a picture of her mother, who had died when Fukuda san was just thirteen. She said she believed what I had told her about salvation, but she knew if she accepted Christ, she'd never see her mother again because she died not knowing the Lord.

We talked about it and read Romans 1, and then I gave her the plan of salvation, and she prayed and asked the Lord into her heart. She was radiant after this time of prayer. We talked on for a while longer about growing in the Lord. She was very happy with all that had taken place.

She missed a couple of *fujinkai*, and it was another few weeks after that when we saw her again. She looked very, very sad, and I was sorry for seeing her this way. She was happiest when she was attending church.

Miyazaki san continued working with her, and Fukuda san told her she wanted to believe all the way. Salvation is one step at a time for a Buddhist. The death of her mother, whom she loved and longed to join, never seeing her again continued to weigh heavy on her heart.

CHAPTER 33

Fighting the Old Ways

Take care, brethren, that there not be any one
of you and evil, unbelieving heart that falls away
from the loving God. But encourage one another
day after day as long as it is called "today," so that
none of you will be hardened by the deceitfulness
of sin.

—Hebrews 3:12–13

One afternoon, Tazaki san told me about a woman in the *danchi* choir who was interested in Christian things. That afternoon, Nakajima san and I went to see her. She was very friendly. We invited her to the first January *fujinkai*, and she was delighted to come.

The next time I saw her, she told me her father had been ill for some time with diabetes, and he was in serious condition. I went to visit with her every opportunity I had. Her father was to have surgery on his liver. The Christians in the group prayed for him, and that greatly impressed Nakamura san.

I really enjoyed her vibrant personality, and she really was a sweet, active, and loving person. She was the means in bringing six other ladies to *fujinkai*, including one who had accepted Christ ten years earlier, but as she admitted later, had been "hiding my head under a bushel." This woman later moved to another area. We tried to connect her with a church in that area, but I don't know if she ever followed up.

I used the lesson of the sower and the seed in Matthew 13 in one *fujinkai*, and afterward, Nakamura san stopped me and said, "Sensei, I am one of the grounds that the sower planted seed in."

She was very concerned, so I asked her if Tazaki san and I could come visit with her, and she readily agreed. We went and had a wonderful visit. We talked about the soil in the lessons, and then I simply gave her the message from the wordless book. She said she wanted to accept the Lord into her heart, and she prayed a beautiful prayer, asking Jesus to forgive her sins and to come into her heart. She was glowing afterward. I saw her a couple of days later, and she still was so happy.

Not long after, she brought her mother to church, but she still had not told her husband about her decision for Christ. We encouraged her to do so, and we prayed about it together. Nakamura san worked for a material shop, testing good and bad material. She also babysat for her daughter's piano teacher, and her husband worked two jobs to make ends meet. She often promised to be in church but conflicted with her job and family. She regularly attended *fujinkai* and the weekly prayer meeting.

Several months passed after she was saved, and while she said she was having problems, she told me she knew she still was saved. I didn't understand why she didn't grasp as much as the other ladies did, but until she let go and let the Lord take over, she would continue to struggle. Later that year, we could still tell that she was fighting the Lord. Her battle with her old life was not letting her to step out for the Lord. And we found out that she still had not told her parents of her decision for Christ.

One day, when Nakajima san and I had gone to visit Nakamura san, she was not home, so we rang the doorbell of a neighbor and invited her to *fujinkai*. She was so happy to be asked, and Nakajima san made arrangements to pick her up. As it worked out, Nakamura san came with Noma san that day with Nakajima san. Noma san then started attending church regularly.

She accepted Christ into her heart a couple of months later, with Tazaki san leading the conversation. Then she started falling off on her church and *fujinkai* attendance. When we would go visit her, she offered many different excuses why she had not been attending. We met her husband, who was a sweet, caring man, and he expressed an interest in attending church as well but said his work schedule was so terrible, he couldn't do it right then.

Those excuses kept coming for some time, and she told us that she was too busy for things of the Lord. We saw her a few months later, and she said that was going to start coming back to church and *fujinkai*. She did and was very open to the things of the Lord.

Noma san was having a difficult time with religious services at the temple. One morning, Roger preached on Elijah and Baal. Noma san was so troubled that she was practically running away from church because she was so troubled. She didn't want to see me. We just prayed that the Lord would have the victory. Six months later, He did. Noma san told me that she had resolved the issues over her old life and longed for a closer walk with Jesus.

Kamimura san was another woman that Nakamura san brought to *fujinkai*, and she showed some interest. She purchased a Bible that first day and said she was really interested in what she heard at *fujinkai* that day.

I went to visit her home, and I met her grandmother, a dear old lady and the last remaining grandparent on both sides of the family. In the home, a *butsudan* (Buddhist god shelf) and *kamidana* (Shinto god shelf) were on full display. Kamimura san talked freely about the idols in her house. At one time, they had been taken out of the home. She really missed them and had been brought back into the home. We prayed that Grandma's heart would allow them to be taken away forever.

Kamimura san was open to the gospel, and we prayed that the Lord would keep her heart soft to the things of the Lord. But there was a fierce spiritual battle going on as her mother-in-law told Kamimura san that she must be Buddhist and take care of the family *butsudan*.

This was a struggle we found in many of our people over the years. Buddhism had been such a strong belief system in Japanese families through the generations. The people with whom we were working often still were tied to the family belief system, and it was difficult for them to let go. They wanted to turn their lives over to the Lord, but family dictated that they stay true to the old ways.

Kamimura san loved to come to our English class, and the class would often turn into a Bible study. She was open to God's love but would freeze when she got home. After months and months of praying for this dear girl and the other women's witnessing to her, she broke down in tears and said she wanted to trust Christ. She said that in her heart, she wanted to but couldn't hurt her mother-in-law. She pleaded with us to understand.

CHAPTER 34

Watanabe San

Let all bitterness and wrath and anger and clamor and slander put away from you, along with all malice. Be kind one to one another, tender-hearted, forgiving each other, just as God in Christ also has forgiven you.

—Ephesians 4:31–32

When Roger saw Watanabe san one Saturday, he asked him if he would be willing to share his testimony in church the next day. Watanabe san was delighted and ready to do so. The next morning, he stood before our congregation, sharing how he became a Christian. He first gave some background to his feelings and literally poured out his heart to us that morning.

As a youth, he said, "It had been drilled into me over and over that America must be destroyed. America was no good. It was the enemy, and we were to do whatever it took to destroy America. I was told that if I ever were to fight for the emperor, I was to blow up the Empire State Building in New York City."

He finished high school about the same time the war ended before he could fight and then went on to college. He enjoyed studying about people, the Jews in particular. An opportunity came along for him to travel to Israel to study. In June 1965, he had traveled by ship from Japan through the Panama Canal then up to New York City before heading on to Israel.

He still maintained a bitter heart against the country that he had once sworn to destroy. He got into a taxi, and in his best English, asked to be taken the Empire State Building. He put both hands on the base of that building and looked up only to find that he could not see the top of the building. It was so huge. At that point, he realized what a complete idiot he had been. His country never would have destroyed that building; he would have been destroyed first. His country was not interested in people, just gain.

He walked up to the third floor and in the men's room stopped in front of the mirror and cried aloud, "What a fool you are, Watanabe!

"There was a terrible battle going on in my body between good and evil," he told us, "and at that point, I decided to find the real answer to peace and began my search. I searched that day and found a home—International Students, Inc.—and went to the office where I met a Mr. Viekman, who, that afternoon, took me to his home. He answered my many questions, and at the end of eight days, I went to my room, got on my knees, and asked Jesus to forgive my sins, cleanse my heart of sin, and come and live in my heart.

"I had left Japan a miserable man, unstable and very unhappy as I left on that ship. After I accepted Jesus in my heart, I was stable, happy, and rejoicing in my new life. But I was just beginning.

"I was told to look up an Arab, a Christian, and he and I had a great fellowship together. Then, while I was in Israel, the Lord opened the heart of one of the Jewish students, and this dear Jew asked Jesus into his heart.

"When I left Israel, I had fifty-two of my students at the port to say farewell, and the hated Arab and Jew were now one in Christ standing arm in arm. This is what the loving Jesus has done."

When he finished his testimony, you could have heard a pin drop. That Sunday and the following, his wife had joined him, but at the time, she was not a believer. They had dinner with us both days, and she started attending *fujinkai* too.

One day, Roger told me that when she left one day after church, she said, "I wanted to say yes. Soon I will."

Roger said she seemed bothered, and we prayed that one day, she would ask Jesus into her heart.

CHAPTER 35

Yui San

Oh taste and see that the Lord is good;
How blessed is the man that takes refuge in Him.

—Psalms 34:8

"Today, I would like to introduce you to a very special friend of mine," Roger started out a sermon one Sunday. "His name is Jesus."

Sitting in church for the first time, these were the words Yui san had ever heard from God's Word. She sat on the edge of her seat really taking every word to heart.

He didn't always give an invitation, but this particular Sunday, he felt led to do so. Four hands were raised as soon as he asked. We talked to each separately that day. Roger and I went to see Yui san that afternoon, and she welcomed us with open arms and unraveled her story for us.

She had been working almost as long as she had been married, but at the end of the previous year, she decided to stop working. Then she started feeling sorry for herself, and she became weary of life and tried many things to bring her joy. She even read three large volumes by the leading psychiatrists in Japan. She devoured the books but found nothing that satisfied her heart.

She went to the top of a high mountain and prayed to a god somewhere to come and show himself and fill her with peace. She returned home, still searching, hunting, and looking for something that she knew she needed, but it did not come. She listened to a volume of records from a Catholic Mass recording. She played them all, but they left her remorseful, not happy. She said her heart craved something, and she was going to find it.

One Sunday morning, she was to go to her daughter's *undokai* (school sports festival) but didn't want to go. She said she had a deep desire to go to church, something she had never done. So she forfeited playing on the mother's team at the *undokai* and went to church.

She told Roger, "The first words you spoke were to me. I wanted your friend."

Before Roger and I left her that evening, she invited Jesus into her heart. We left a Bible with her to read, and she told us later she read it all evening and understood what she read. The next morning, she read more. Her heart was filled with joy as she read on. She shared her experience with Nakajima san on Monday. Tuesday night, her heart was filled with such happiness in being invited to *fujinkai*. A smile from Tazaki san and I gave her the added encouragement she needed to know that she was wanted and loved.

Wednesday, Ginny Jahnke from our home office spoke during *fujinkai* on J-O-Y—"put Jesus and Others ahead of You," and you will have eternal joy. She said it was another message just for her, and she felt blessed by the realness of the week and rejoiced in the Lord.

A couple weeks later, during our share time at the ladies' prayer meeting, she told us that she has her own room and her husband another. Her concern was that she didn't know if she really loved him, and she longs for real love for her family, that they also will come to Jesus, whom she now has come to know and love.

Little by little, she came to understand real love. Jesus's love was so real to her. Yui san found that real peace in the Lord in precious. She said she was a new person and is happy in so many ways.

Her husband was transferred for his job to another area, and we encouraged her to attend Domei Church, which she did. She later told me that she had started a women's Bible study at her new church.

CHAPTER 36

Yoda San

Behold, I am the Lord, the God of all flesh; is anything too difficult for me?

—Jeremiah 32:27

Yoda san started coming to church in October 1966. She raised her hand on Christmas Day that year to make a commitment to Christ. Roger and I went to see her the following Tuesday. She had been one of the hardest people to reach. We have seen the power of the evil one on folks but not like we did December 27.

We arrived at her apartment that afternoon, and she was all ready for us. We were greeted at the door by four lively children, two of her own and two of her sister-in-law's children. The kids had been primed to be good when sensei was there, and they had promised to behave. The little room was opened to them, and they were given a large bowl of *mikan* (Mandarin oranges). They also had all sorts of games with which to play. We sat with a *kotatsu* (a thick warm quilt under which people sat to keep warm) to talk and teach her God's Word.

The noise in the apartment soon reached a level I will never forget. The four children were so loud. Roger talked on to her, and her ears were all tuned to what he was saying. She seemed oblivious to the noise in the apartment. At times, you could barely hear Roger's voice, but she continued to listen carefully to his words. We were looking to the Word of God for help along the way. It was amazing.

I found myself really talking to the Lord about the noise because it was so loud. The wordless book was explained, and when it came time to pray, Yoda san was more than willing. As Roger prayed and was about to finish, the telephone rang and rang and rang. I thought she would get up and answer it because it was so *nigiyaka* (noisy), but she started to pray. The phone rang again, the television was turned on, and the children started singing.

I got up to answer the phone. "*Mushi, mushi* [hello]?" I said, but there was no one there.

Yoda san was still praying, confessing her sins, and asking Jesus into her life. It was a precious and sweet moment. The kids, and the television screamed on.

As I prayed in closing, the phone started ringing again, but Yoda san did not get up to answer it. I heard her oldest son answer the phone, "*Mushi, mushi?*" He slammed it back down and yelled, "*Dare mo imasen* (there was no one there)," and he was disgusted.

As I said, "Amen," and Roger and Yoda san each added their amen, total silence reigned. Literally, the television went off, the four kids had their coats on, and they went outside to play, and after the door slammed shut, silence.

Jesus was the victor. It was that plain. No more battle. He had won it at that point, and we really praised the Lord. We talked about the Christian life for another hour. It was such a thrilling afternoon, and just as we finished talking and were drinking tea, the little ones came back in.

She told us several weeks later that she had spent time witnessing to her husband, sister-in-law, and brother-in-law, and there didn't seem to be any opposition, except her husband used to play golf on Sundays, but the weather turned cold, and he hadn't played but seemed to pick arguments with her to keep her home on Sunday mornings. She has had discipline problems with her boys. She says they are naughty, but they are boys and will be all right. For a while it seemed they were sick on days she was planning to attend *fujinkai*.

One prayer meeting, she did ask if she should continue to pray at the *butsudan* (god shelf) in her home. I was surprised to hear that, but I had not even thought about this being a problem to her, but it was. Another woman at prayer meeting that day said she had problems with the paper prayers. Buddhists will write their prayers on slips of paper and tie them onto string at the local temple. This woman said she was told to get rid of them because the true God would take care of her needs.

Yoda san said she didn't put rice and water on the shelf, and she didn't pray to the gods of the shelf, but all her life, she was in the habit of praying there, so she now goes there to pray to the one true God. She said she wasn't sure if that was the right thing to do. We prayed with her about it, and the next prayer meeting, she told us that she no longer prayed to God at the *butsudan*.

CHAPTER 37

The Okada Family

These things I have spoken to you, so that in Me
you may have peace. In the world you have tribulations, but take courage; I have overcome the
world.

—John 16:33

I didn't know what the man at the door wanted at first. It took another worker from the New Life League printing facility to help me understand that this man wanted Roger to take a funeral. At first, Roger didn't know what to say since the man was not a Christian, but as the story came out about the accident, he felt that he should do this. It proved to be a wonderful opportunity for the Lord.

Okada san's youngest daughter had been hit and killed by a train. Roger met with the family and found them to be very open and loving. He told them right away that if they had a Christian funeral, it would do nothing for the child to get into heaven, as she was already dead. Buddhists believe that they can do a variety of things to help the dead get into heaven. Roger wanted to make that very clear, and they agreed.

We had never been to a Buddhist funeral, but they are very solemn and so pathetic because they have no hope without the Lord Jesus Christ. They have a "laying away" ceremony the night before the funeral. When Roger walked in that next morning, he told me the girl's body was lying there on her futon right in front of where they were talking. She had been there since the accident, and he said it was pretty strange.

That night was the laying away ceremony, where the family would place the little girl's body in a pine box and then have a ceremony. However, since they asked Roger to take care of all the arrangements, he told them they could put her in the box and fix up the room only with real flowers. Usually, there were all kinds of artificial flowers for a Buddhist funeral. The family said they would do as he said.

We went back later that night with Tazaki san, Ona san, Miyamoto san, Suga san, and Kitahara san from our church. We did not know what they would have done, but we found the room where the girl's body had been lying was beautiful. The pine box still was there, but they also had draped the room with black cloth, and on that cloth was a gold embossed cross. On the pine box was a live flower cross, and that was all.

It was very lovely. The mother was so sweet and so grateful for all that Roger had done. He gave the family the words of life and talked about their need of accepting Christ because that is what little Yukari chan would have wanted. The service didn't take long, but it was really sweet. We all sang some hymns, and then after a while, Roger took some of the church folks home before returning to the Okada home. They had insisted we stay for the family gathering where they traditionally bring out a feast. It really was a feast and all was delicious.

Before Roger returned, it felt odd sitting there with a family we barely knew during such a sad time, but they seemed to appreciate our being there, and so we talked about the Lord. Miyamoto san and I did most of the talking. When Roger returned, he drank some tea, ate some food, and then we all left.

We had Sunday school and church the next morning, hurried through a light lunch before heading out to the funeral. There were a lot of people there from the neighborhood, friends and family from near and far. Many of the church folks attended as well. That was wonderful and a testimony to the family, too. Yukari chan's class-mates attended too.

I knew that I would not soon forget that service and the impact it had on the hearts of our church people. I really saw those without the Lord in agony, and it was terrible. Many in attendance were just sobbing and sobbing and had nothing to help them. How very happy I was that we had hope for the future through Jesus Christ.

We stayed until the hearse came and took the family to the crematorium. They wanted us to go too, but that was the last night of some special tent meetings we had been having in the *danchi*, so we couldn't go.

The following Sunday, the Okada family was in church for the first time in their lives. As the hymns were sung, and especially "The Love of God," which had been sung at the funeral, Mrs. Okada's eyes filled with tears. Each Sunday after that, the family would be in church, and each week, they seemed more relaxed and more intent to understand. Christmas Day, she brought lunch, and they stayed at the church until the Sunday school program started.

The Sunday before Christmas, Mr. Okada brought and planted five lovely rose bushes for me, and after time, they bloomed with beautiful flowers. They were always doing some act of kindness. When an offering was taken for the church building fund, they dropped a large contribution in the offering.

Just before Christmas, Mr. Okada came to our annual party at the house and then went caroling with some of the young folks and really seemed to enjoy the time. The family seemed very interested in the ways of the Lord, but it was new to a family that had been raised in the ways of Buddhism. We continued to pray for their salvation.

The following July, Mr. Okada became ill and was taken to the hospital. He apparently had been ill for some time, but doctors had just found cancer in his kidneys. In October that year, he was up and about, changing his room, ate all three meals that day, and seemed to be enjoying himself. The next day, he fell into a coma in the morning and didn't respond to treatment.

The doctors worked all day and night to relieve him of the pain he was suffering but were unable to do much. The doctors said it was just a matter of time since kidney cancer was terminal. He did come back out of the coma and his wife was able to visit. She brought him a Bible, and she took the opportunity to witness to him and to tell him about the things of the Lord that she knew. He did read over and over the places that he finally understood.

Mrs. Okada called and said the doctors had done all they could and that her husband would die soon. We went to visit with them at the hospital. On the way to the hospital, we felt that we would just be visiting a man on his deathbed, but on the way home that night, we felt we had met with a man who had accepted Christ and had a new outlook.

CHAPTER 38

More Victories for Christ

I have been crucified with Christ; and it is no longer I who live, but Christ lives in me; and the life which I now live in the flesh I live by faith in the Son of God, who loved me and gave Himself up for me.

—Galatians 2:20

When we left for Japan in 1951, we went with faith that the Lord would provide for us, protect us, and lead us to the work that He wanted us to perform. The Lord was faithful and blessed our work many times over, many times more than we could even imagine.

From the early converts while we were in Hachioji to those who became believers through the tent meetings to the men and women in the *danchi* who accepted Christ as their Savior, the Lord worked through us in ways we couldn't even think possible when we started. But we believed in the Lord and trusted Him. Our goal still was to work ourselves out of job having national workers take over the responsibilities of the church. Some came and believed; others came but didn't believe and left. These are some of those stories.

* * * * *

Okubo san came to the house one day in October, looking for a church to call home. She was wholeheartedly interested in finding a home church. After attending another church, she met Miyazaki san, who told her about our church, and a couple weeks later, she showed up for prayer meeting, her children in tow. I didn't really know where she stood, but she did tell me that she had never been to a church before and was not a Christian. She continued to attend prayer meetings, seeking God's will for her life. Things changed the end of November.

At prayer meeting, Miyazaki san, Nakajima san, Nakano san, Nishimoto san, and Shimoyoshi san had prayed; we waited for Okubo san. She started praying and then began to cry as she poured out her heart to the Lord and confessed her sin and her desire for Jesus to come and clean her heart. Her lack of patience and lack of love all distressed her, and her short temper made her realize that she needed Jesus.

Soon after, she started working in the Sunday school in the little children's class and became a blessing to the program.

* * * * *

Hiyabashi san had been attending church and Sunday school for about two years. She had gone through the motions of salvation, but she attended a Bible camp during the summer one year and really decided to let go for Jesus. She read on in her Bible and decided to be baptized.

Her mother and father both said, "No," because they were both Soka Gakkai, a Buddhist sect, but Hiyabashi san prayed on. She finally asked Roger and Miyamoto san to visit her parents, but instead, her mother came to church late but talked about what was taking place.

After several weeks, her parents finally gave permission for her to be baptized, and her mother even attended the ceremony. It was a lovely service, and Hiyabashi san gave a sweet testimony of the grace of the Lord in her life.

* * * * *

We received in the mail a signed decision card following a Billy Graham Crusade meeting and Roger called the number immediately to invite Itoh san to church that morning. He was grateful for the call, but his daughter had presented him with his first grandson that morning, and he was going to the hospital to see the baby and his daughter before returning to another Billy Graham meeting at Korakuen (a sports stadium), and he would be in church the following week.

He arrived with a friend in tow, an Aoki san. It was a welcome sight to see these two men, and I encouraged him to bring his wife the following week. He did, and we spent the afternoon with them and got to know them quite well. They also introduced us to some good friends, and we had a great time talking about the Lord and praying for the baby. They attended church regularly, and we kept praying for their salvation.

* * * * *

Tonikura san came to *fujinkai* and told me at the end of the class that she had not understood any of the things I had talked about and would not be back. I encouraged her to come back, but she seemed so hard and uninterested.

Akiko san told me later that Tonikura san had tried to find peace, but without success. She prayed faithfully at the *butsudan* (god shelf) in her home every day, and when the worship was over, she had nothing. So several weeks later, she tried smoking, and when that didn't bring her inner peace, she started drinking *sake* (rice wine) because it seemed to help others. She was seeking real help and had not found it.

We kept praying that she would find the peace she so desperately was seeking. There is such peace in the Lord, if she only knew.

* * * * *

The Makinos came to church on a Christmas Eve for the very first time. They seemed very interested and said they would return. Nakano san and I called on them many times over the next several months, and they finally returned to church in June. Roger made it a point to get to know this couple, and it turned out they may have met years earlier. Mr. Makino first heard the gospel at the Ginza Methodist Church at a GI Gospel Hour program. Roger and his buddy Dub Jackson helped get those meetings started in the fall of 1945 while they were still stationed in Tokyo right after the war.

What a great joy it was to find out this man found the Lord through that witness. They both started attending church regularly, with Mr. Makino praying for his wife to come to the Lord.

* * * * *

Sato san became a Christian after hearing Roger explain to a friend of hers the plan of salvation. She had been attending one of our English classes and then Bible study when Roger was talking to her friend. Her friend was saved that night, but Sato san said she was not yet ready. She did keep coming to English class and the Bible study. Weeks passed before she decided to put her trust in the Lord.

Later, we talked with her about baptism, and she was ready for that next step, but one of our coworkers informed us that she still had a *butsudan* in her home. After one Bible study, Roger, and I talked with her about the *butsudan*. I asked who was taking care of it. She smiled and said, "No one since I accepted the Lord. It's not a problem to me, just that her testimony will be upheld to her sister with whom she lived."

Both of their parents were dead, and Roger had the joy of giving her sister the plan of salvation. Sato san burned the *butsudan* after her sister too accepted Christ.

To raise money for our church building fund, we passed out "banks" for our church people to fill. Sato san tried to think of a way to fill her bank but kept coming up blank. So she asked God to help her have some money for the church building. Soon after, her boss asked her to do something she had never done before, and when she got paid for it, she felt certain it was for the church fund and gave it. What a thrilling testimony, and we praised the Lord for this work in her heart.

* * * * *

Hiyashi san gave Marusugi san and me a royal welcome when we went to visit in her home. She graciously served coffee and seemed genuinely happy that we had come. I found an open heart. She attended our next *fujinkai*. I loaned her my Japanese New Testament, and she was grateful. She turned to Ueno san, the friend who had introduced us, and said, "Why did you not tell me about this before?"

She didn't miss many meetings and attended church regularly. Her daughter Noriko chan was a leader in our Sunday school and was delighted that her mother was attending church.

Then a few months later, attendance for both of them became irregular until they both stopped attending altogether. When we went to visit, Hiyashi san gave us nothing but excuses. Finally, several months later again, she asked us to stop bothering her about church.

We kept praying for this family. While we don't know what ultimately happened, we do know that a seed was planted, and the Lord was in control.

CHAPTER 39

The Church Building the Church a Building

> What is the outcome then, brethren? When you
> assemble, each one has a psalm, has a teaching,
> has a revelation, has a tongue, has an interpreta-
> tion. Let all things be done for edification.
>
> —1 Corinthians 14:26

Tent meetings had gone by the wayside for the most part as a way to bring the gospel to the people, but we wanted to show the people of our church the power of the Lord to reach sinners. As a church, we decided to have a series of tent meetings in the *danchi*. Some of our people were skeptical about what could be done, but they moved forward by faith. We couldn't actually have it in the *danchi*, but we secured a piece of land on the edge of the *danchi* to erect a twenty-foot-by-forty-foot heavy canvas tent, run electricity to the tent, and to hold three nights of meetings. There were so many little things that needed to be done, and as busy as our church folks were already, they stepped up.

Nishimoto san's house was opened up for prayer meeting. She invited her neighbors in for a Bible study and prayer meeting. Eleven of us were there, including several of her neighbors. It was a thrilling opportunity to give them the gospel—John 3:16–18. The wordless book was sort of explained, but it whet their appetite to attend the tent meetings.

The first day of the tent meetings was fine weather-wise. The tent was put up, grass in the area was mowed, and benches needed to be assembled. Three storms were in the area that night. We didn't know who, if anyone, would show up that first night. But we went ahead and placed the benches and chairs because we knew this was God's work and His will, so we prayed that His will would be done.

We worked hard all day and were so tired, but we held a prayer meeting at Goto san's house, and then we had a practice for the ladies quartet that would be performing. We ordered dinner for all who had helped set up.

At 6:30 that evening, the lights blew out, and Roger spent the next hour trying to figure out the problem. Our signs in the *danchi* were destroyed by the wind. To make matters even more difficult, there were to be two *undokai* (school sports festival), so parents had to let their children sleep and could not leave them home alone.

When the first night of meetings began, the tent was full. All nineteen benches plus twenty chairs were full of adults, and others were standing inside as well as outside the tent. What a thrill to see the tent overflowing capacity.

The youth choir sang their hearts out, testimonies were shared, the film we had scheduled was well received, and Murase san's message was very good. He was building his message over the three nights of meetings, so we didn't know who would be coming back to hear the second and third parts.

Saturday broke as a gloomy, rainy day. We really didn't know about attendance that night. We held an impromptu prayer meeting with several of our church folks, giving thanksgiving to the Lord for what He had done the night before, and praised Him for His goodness.

That night, I picked up several people in our car, and when we walked into the tent, we found a trough full of muddy water, but it was a place where hearts were hungry for the Word of God. The youth choir sang again, and the violinist we scheduled played such sweet music. Murase san's message was as good that second night, focusing on filling with a need for the folks to need Jesus.

With the storms still blowing around, after that second night we decided to fold down the tent so it wouldn't be damaged. Large trees had fallen, and there were three inches of water on the ground. But the meetings had to go on, and they did.

That third night, even after feeling the brunt of the storms, the benches and chairs were filled and people standing filled the rest of the tent and then even more outside. The music and the message touched their hearts. Murase san's final message made the Lord come alive in that tent. Many in attendance wanted to know more about the Lord, and a few even made decisions for Jesus that night.

The church folks had done most of the work to the best of their ability, and we heard over and over how the tent meetings were "homegrown," and we praised the Lord for everything.

Little did we know at that time that event was just the beginning of the church people working together. The Lord was preparing them for something even bigger. God had grown a church in the *danchi*; it was time to build a permanent home. Little by little, we were getting to the place where we needed a building of our own because we had outgrown the small building where we had been meeting. Our baptistery, a concrete block tank that Roger had built beneath the floor in the church, was in dire need of repair. We needed land and a building to hold our growing congregation.

Our house, which was near to the church building, was where Sunday school was held for the children. They met in Tim's and Gary's bedrooms, the high school kids in the living room, and the junior high kids in Roger's office. We were pushing out the walls in both the house and the office building where we held church services. It was time to build the church a building.

In 1967, we had a dollar come in a Christmas card with a note to tell "Uncle Roger" to use it toward the building of God's church. That Christmas, Roger used that dollar bill to teach the people a new term—"faith promise" giving. Some said it was impossible, but we know God is the God of the impossible. That faith promise offering brought seven hundred dollars into the offering bags. It was such a wonderful Sunday. We had received several thousand dollars in the mail to be used for the church to be built.

Land was expensive. Our funds were small for the cost, but the men searched and found a small parcel of ground in a pretty good location near the *danchi*. The mission had some money come in allocated for a new church, and it was given to us for land. We were excited as the landowner came to sign the papers, but when he arrived, our Japanese land committee was saddened to hear the man say, "Sorry, sensei, the land I promised you is in the midst of new housing, and when the neighbors, whose sun comes from the south, heard about the church, they really complained that their heat for the winter would be blocked and would make their homes cold."

I heard the men say, "Oh, no," and they talked on. Decisions had to be made. We had come too far to have this disappointment.

Before too much discussion continued, the landowner said, "But, sensei, I do have another piece of land at the end of the housing area. It is next to an area where houses can never be built because of an extensive radio antenna system. It is about one twentieth of an acre, is a little more expensive, and I can show it to you now."

The new excitement of this new possible piece of land made the land committee rejoice and praise the Lord because the second location was far better than the first. It was a real prayer time around the table that day. The men stepped out by faith to make up the difference in the price of the land. As they prayed, God already was at work. The money needed soon was in hand and the papers were signed. Not long after that, we held a groundbreaking ceremony, Japanese style, and it was quite exciting.

The leaders in the church decided it was time for committees to be formed. There was a light fixture committee, a furniture committee, a building design committee, a color committee, etc. Roger and I knew the church had to be theirs with their decisions. No one wanted to be left out of the planning and decision-making process. Even seekers were included. No one was left out. Young and old were involved in the process. A miracle was taking place. It was all part of God's plan.

Sunday after signing the papers was a day of great rejoicing. Roger's message that day was full of power as he spoke on faith. Faith is what we needed because we did not have all the money necessary to construct the building, but we knew God was in charge, and by faith, He would see us through.

No one had any architectural experience. When Roger had said, "Church design," no one had any idea what a church should look like. They had to conduct research to see what a church looked like and what should be included in the building. It had to be their design, fit the needs of their church, and include space for a pastor's house, all in one twentieth of an acre. We prayed for God's design. It was amazing what came out of discussions when the sensei was quiet.

Where to put the toilet was a big concern. To the Japanese, the bathroom is always at the entrance. We kept quiet and waited. The pros and the cons started coming out. What to do next? With two stories, where would the Sunday school be located, upstairs or downstairs? How many seats do we want, fifty? We were already beyond that. One hundred? What colors do we want inside and on the roof? What kind of window sash, aluminum or wood? Do we want carpeted or tiled floors?

Oh, the committees worked hard. The church was to suit their needs. Sensei would not be there after it was built. The Japanese pastor, our coworker, would be in charge. Yes, God was at work.

Once the church people had the design of the church in mind, Roger made a model out of balsa wood to scale and took it to an architect asking for blueprints. The architect said it was a very sound design with no need for improvements. Blueprints were made.

People in the church, for the most part, performed much of the construction on the building. It was not unusual to see women of the church mixing sand, gravel, water, and cement in a small mixer we purchased to make mortar for the block construction. Some women who had babies or were expecting, kept us supplied with cake, cookies, fruit, ice cream, and beverages. Our cookie box was never empty.

Roger, men in the church, even our Tim and Gary spent many hours working on all of the various parts of the construction. Roger did the block laying, electrical, plumbing, and painting. It took vacations and holidays for some of the men to work, but when they did work, a great deal was accomplished. We did pay for Japanese crews to erect the steel skeleton of the building, to put on the roof, as well as a stonemason for the rockwork. What a thrill it was to watch the steel frame go up. Roger told one of our young people that he knew how a mother must feel after waiting nine months for a baby to be born and then to see the actual form for the first time.

When the window spaces were finished, every aluminum sash had to be custom cut to size. Roger and I spent a night cutting and fitting every window—all twenty-two of them—and we were weary when morning came.

Roger struggled trying to figure out how to make a staircase between floors that would not take up a lot of room. One morning, he came to breakfast with the solution that he said God gave to him in a dream—a circular staircase that would fit in one corner and not take up a lot of space. And that's what he built.

As the church was being built, money was coming in from all over to help pay for the construction, sometimes even before we asked. The Japanese sacrificed money they had been saving for a new house. It was thrilling to hear of some who prayed all night for funds to come in.

An overseas caller said, "I had no intention of calling you today, but for some reason, the burden came over me. I just sent some money to the mission office for the building."

They did not know until we had talked on the phone that we had used up all the sand and gravel and had no money to continue. The men had been in the other room, praying for the funds to come in. By the time we got to work the next morning, sand and gravel had been ordered. We didn't miss one day.

To keep expenses down, the pews were made in a prison wood-working shop according to our design. The pulpit and communion table came from the same source. The concrete blocks for the walls were made in another prison.

Everyone was praying. We found out from a missionary friend that a hotel in Tokyo was replacing its lobby carpet, and we were able to get a large portion. All we had to do was rent a truck to get it hauled.

The building was taking shape, and most importantly, it was their building. The mission sent Roger to Singapore as construction on the church was nearing an end. Evangelistic meetings were to be held to dedicate the building when he returned. Again, the church people planned it all.

Our Japanese pastor and his bride and the people in the church had everything arranged. The people worked out all the details. It was exciting to see Japanese flower arrangements arrayed throughout the building. Refreshment tables spread with a feast were ready for after the ceremony. Invitations had been sent out. The church was mobbed to overflowing. What a wonderful day of rejoicing. The building, two stories high, had a peaked roof with a lighted cross reaching toward the heavens.

All during the construction, a neighborhood woman would come and watch us work nearly every day. She came to church that first Sunday the building was finished and accepted Christ shortly thereafter.

Sunday school on clear days was held outside of the new building but was overjoyed when they were told even though the building was incomplete at the time, they would be having church school on the first floor. One of the elders had his business office men help move the piano into the church schoolroom, and kids could be heard singing for miles around. I can still hear Papa Tazaki saying to his friends as they carried the piano into the building, "This is our church. The Lord provided for it each step of the way."

That first Sunday, the church school was pushing the walls out. Junior high and high school–aged kids met upstairs in the sanctuary. Could anything be more exciting?

With each new child, it meant a new mother and father to contact, and visitation became another important step in the growth of the church. Our goal was to have an indigenous church, and that meant working ourselves out of a job. Just as the church people created the various committees to build the church, they also planned not just for the evangelism meetings, but they also shared the responsibility for cleaning and maintaining the building. All were involved in its upkeep. It was theirs, and they had been a part of it.

We started construction of the church in March 1968, and we finished in November that year. The building was finished, the pastor had been called, and we left it in their very capable hands when we returned to the US in December that year.

CHAPTER 40

Nishibori Fukuin Kyokai Flourishes

So the churches were being strengthened in the
faith, and were increasing in numbers daily.

—Acts 16:5

In 1968, Roger and I were called back to the States to be area representatives for the mission board to recruit young people to go to Japan to be church planters. We moved back to Mesa, Arizona, to the home we had purchased in 1961.

Roger spent many weeks each year traveling around the southwestern part of America, visiting churches and colleges, meeting with and encouraging young people to become missionaries. It was satisfying work, and we did that for the next nine years. All during that time, we kept in close contact with our dear Japanese friends at *Nishibori Fukuin Kyokai* (Nishibori Gospel Church).

Nine years later, we did return to Japan for a three-year term. In those years, Roger served as area vice director, evangelism coordinator for SEND. He researched new areas and placed four couples where churches now are established.

As a special joy, he had the privilege, with another missionary, of building the pastor's house at the church as we had envisioned those many years before. We saw a "daughter" church start with the folks from the *danchi* doing all the legwork. It was a wonderful three years.

CHAPTER 41

Church Planting

Be anxious for nothing, but in everything by prayer and supplication with thanksgiving let your requests be made known to God.

—Philippians 4:6

C hurch planting begins with homework. A year or two can be wasted if you don't know where you will be living or what you are going to be doing. It is important to select two or three areas where you desire before the Lord to see the church established. Find out all about the area and jot down all the things that you have discovered. For example, modes of transportation need to be identified. Where is the most people traffic? Are there churches in the area and what kind? Is there room for another church?

Gather maps and population statistics that can be of value to you. Find out if the men are factory workers, or are they business or government workers? On a large city map, lay out the church locations and put a pin in the center of the area. If there are churches, visit the pastors and invite them to lunch. Will they be offended that you want to come to their area to work? Do they feel that it would be good to have a foreigner in the area? What can you offer them in the way of service to enhance the whole ministry for the Lord?

Find out all you can about the other churches and what their goals are for the future of the city. Are they a Bible-teaching church or not? You soon will see whether or not there is a need for you in the area. At the same time, make a friend of the other pastors and let them know you are interested in the other churches and their ministry without making them feel that you are coming in to "take over their territory."

Get a slow look by riding through the area on a bicycle, and you will find out a great deal about the community. If the population is more than ten thousand and there is just one tiny church, you know that you will not overwhelm the pastor on the existing church. The larger the area, the better your welcome will be. In the *danchi* where we worked, there were no existing churches, and that made it easy to get things going.

Prayer is the key to the work of starting a church. Identify as many as you know who will be praying that you need them to lay the foundation of the upcoming church. God's guidance is so necessary to the work.

After riding through an area and getting to know the community a bit, you will be able to determine who you want to reach. If you are in a highly educated area, then you will want to work with them. They will be able to reach all the area with the message of the Lord if they come to Him.

If you are going to spend all your time with the storekeepers, you will find that their hours will vary from one day to another. You will find that they do not have the free time necessary for the work because they are working long hours each day. You will have to structure a time to go into the store when there are no customers. That is a whole area in the cities that are difficult to reach for the Lord.

You will find in other areas too that some everyday workers reached such as road workers who are laying concrete and could care less about learning English. You will have to use your imagination and a lot of prayer to reach these people too.

The key is to look your city over and think through with whom you want to work and how do your abilities fit in the program of the Lord reaching these for Christ. If your gifts lie in teaching the road workers, then concentrate on them. If your abilities lie in teaching English as a way to reach people, then start with English classes.

Let them know up front that you are there to tell them about the Lord—English lesson first, then a Bible lesson in their language. Never assume anything. Don't let them think one thing when your goal really is to reach them for the Lord.

Let your face be seen everywhere. Get in with the women. At different times in Japan, I joined a flower-display class, a Japanese-character brush-writing class, a wood carving class, a doll-making class, and a tea ceremony class. Some of the things may be foreign to you, but these are ways to get in with the people.

Find out what the men like to do in their spare time, and if you do not have to compromise your stand for the Lord, see if they will let you join in. You may like to play golf and can find a group of men that like to play, but be prepared for any expenses that may accompany hobbies such as golf.

The women may be interested in you and in your way of raising your children. They also may be interested in learning how to prepare Western meals. You could start a class on childcare or a Western-style cooking class. Never lose sight of why you are there in the first place—telling them about the Lord Jesus.

Think through some of the lessons you will be bringing and give an outline and main points to whet their appetites for more of what you are trying to tell them. Write a series of messages geared toward each member of the family—father, mother, or kids.

Let them know you are interested in the whole family. Be willing to share your home with them and invite them for a meal or even a party and have lots of fun games that can be played in any language. Invite your neighbors and then the next time invite them to bring a family in whom they are interested. If you have a car at your disposal, perhaps offer to take a pregnant mother to doctor appointments or even the hospital when the baby is arriving.

Begin visitation in the community and try to bring a friend along. It can even be someone who attends a church in another area. It will give your friend an opportunity to share what they believe until you have some fruit in the city in which you are working. It is good to take a national with you for they will be able to get the feel of the thoughts and can tell you where the interest lies in the home. As you become known in the community, you will be able to tell what kind of fruit there will be. You want good fruit for the Lord. You will find some hearts that will be very open to the gospel and will accept the Word of the Lord right away. Sometimes you will find it takes time to see any results for the Lord.

I liken fruit in Japan to the *kaki* (persimmon). There are two types of *kaki*. One is oval and is peeled to eat; the other is long and skinny and is only used for drying. The first is watched with careful eyes to see at what moment it is to be picked, and then it is picked at its peak of ripeness. If it is not picked at just the right time, it will fall to the ground and be squashed and is worth nothing. The long skinny variety of *kaki* is allowed to ripen then gathered all at once, strung on thread, then hung to dry under the eaves of the house until winter sets in. You dip that variety in a bean curd powder before eating them.

Both are delicious, yet the growing time is important to the fruit. The heart of the *kaki* tree is ebony and is more like a person than any other tree for it has a black heart. You want to be a careful fruit picker and be ready for the fruit to fall at just the right time.

As you see the fruit coming along, then you will be able to tell when the church should be started. You will have been having Bible classes coming along and from all levels of society, and then as you get the feel of what they want to do, you let them start making key decisions. Little by little, the church that God started through your work becomes their church, and it will become a national-run-and-supported church.

If there are Christians in the area who have come from different churches and have not grown much since they left that previous church, you will be working to strengthen them in their walk with the Lord. Now it is time to share with new babes in the church what it is all about and introduce them to the Apostle's Creed. It will give them something to hang on to in what they believe.

The Apostles' Creed

I believe in God, the Father almighty, maker of heaven and earth.
I believe in Jesus Christ, His only Son, our Lord, who was conceived by the Holy Spirit born of the virgin Mary, suffered under Pontius Pilate, was crucified, died, and was buried.
He descended into hell.
The third day he rose again from the dead.
He ascended into heaven and is seated at the right hand of God the Father almighty.
From there he will come to judge the living, and the dead.
I believe in the Holy Spirit, the holy Christian Church, the communion of saints, the forgiveness of sins, the resurrection of the body, and the life everlasting. Amen.

The Apostles' Creed is not found in the Bible. It is the work of early Christians who wanted to create a summary, based on various Bible passages, to explain to others what it means to be a Christian.

Begin them right away in a Bible memory course, perhaps one that you have created. Explain the meaning of baptism and communion ahead of time and let them think through what they want to do about it. As they grow in the Lord, they will begin to discern more and more of the Biblical teachings. Let them know they belong to a large family in Christ. They will be a part of the body of the Lord and of these Christians all over the world.

Always encourage them to tell their family members what they are doing so that they do not separate themselves from their natural families. It may be necessary to only baptize them when they have received permission from family members. You will want to spend time in the home of the new believer and share with the rest of the family that you are not there to sever relationships but to unite the family.

From the beginning, introduce them to missionary work. Tell them that you are a missionary in their country, and there are missionaries sharing the gospel of Christ with people all around the world. Let missions become a part of the church from the very beginning and teach them how to give to the Lord's work. It will all be very new to them. Let them know where is their Jerusalem, their Judea, their Samaria.

> But you shall receive power when the Holy Spirit
> has come upon you and you shall be My witnesses
> both in Jerusalem, and in all Judea and Samaria, and
> even to the remotest part of the earth. (Acts 1:8)

After you have seen a bit of "fruit" from your efforts, take a babe with you to do visitation, and if they are willing, have them share what the Lord has done for them. Firsthand testimonies are so important, not only to the person hearing the testimony but to the one giving their testimony. Find something for each to do who comes through for the Lord.

Over the years, we tried many different ways to reach the Japanese. We stuffed envelopes for the letters going out to seekers. We took flyers to our local newspaper. We handed out tracts on street corners and delivered them to people's homes. As our Christian friends grew, we had them plan some of the evangelistic meetings we held. We encouraged our folks to use their talents of flower arranging, leading the singing, saying a prayer, or reading the scripture. We wanted everyone involved and let them take turns.

As a missionary and church planter, you are trying to work yourself out of a job. You want members of the church to eventually take over the responsibilities of the church, its outreach and support. As the group grows in prayer and Bible study, you need to let them know that you will not be with them all the while and that you will be leaving in time and that a national pastor is necessary for the ongoing growth of the work.

You do not want them to be a flock of sheep without a shepherd. If you get to construction of a church building or if the best option is moving into an existing building, make sure that all are involved in the process, as well as the spiritual growth of the church, praying and helping others where they can for those who may be weak in the faith.

CHAPTER 42

Japan Still Needs Missionaries

Then He said to His disciples, "The harvest is plentiful, but the workers are few. Therefore beseech the Lord of the harvest to send out workers into His harvest."

—Matthew 9:37–38

When we returned to Japan in 1978 for three years of service, Kishimoto san was one of the teenagers during the time of our *danchi* work in Higashikurume. He accepted Christ as his Savior and was baptized. He had become a young man, married, and served as an elder in his church in another area of Japan outside of Tokyo. He was working for the government and was in charge of laying out new cities. At that time, he was laying out seven new cities with ten-year projections of having between fifty thousand and 250,000 people.

Each city will be different in population. Most of the men used these cities as bedroom communities until they had enough money saved to move closer to the job and/or to buy a house.

Kishimoto san pleaded with us to come and start some churches in each area. "Sensei," he said, "your mission needs to buy some land now so that when people move in you already will have a beginning." He had wanted so badly to go into full-time Christian work, but his father put such strong pressure on him that he went to college and earned his degree in urban planning. His heart still was burdened for the people of his country.

Kishimoto san's words "come back" still ring in my ears, and I know in time and with the right leadership, churches will be planted in the areas that Kishimoto san was talking about. There are unlimited areas all around Japan that still need to hear the gospel. There are high school–age and college-age young people in Japan that need to hear of the saving grace of Jesus. There are young families and older families that need Jesus.

And there are as many ways to bring them the gospel as you can imagine. But you have to first believe, and then trust in the Lord, and great works can be accomplished because Jesus never fails.

EPILOGUE

Editor's note: I am Gary, Roger and Margaret's youngest mentioned earlier in this book. The genesis of this book was based on a college term paper on "church planting" Mom was writing for a class at Arizona College of the Bible. Well, thirty plus years later, we still are working on the book, and because time does not stand still, it would seem logical that some of the methodology of working on the field had changed from the time Mom and Dad were in Japan to now. While the message of salvation has remained the same, strategies for reaching the unsaved have changed, as have the people who are going out as missionaries today.

* * * * *

Jon Reasoner was a boyhood friend of mine in Japan. The name will sound familiar as he is the son of Rollie and Esther Reasoner and grandson of Shirley and Mannon Reasoner, previously mentioned in these pages.

Jon and his wife Chieko have worked in Okinawa and Japan for several decades. The first twelve years they served as a "cooperating missionaries" with Japanese pastors. Each term on the field, they focused on a different little church, coming alongside the pastor to encourage and to stimulate thinking about how to reach the community for the growth of that church.

Then SEND transferred them to a Japanese church northwest of Tokyo, where they worked for years as pastor of Tokorozawa Megumi Kyokai, a Japanese church planted earlier by SEND missionaries. Their goal was to bring the church to the place where it could call its own Japanese pastor. As their retirement started to approach, they knew that goal would not be met and transferred the leadership of the church in 2015 to other SEND missionaries.

In general, Jon told me SEND International is emphasizing the making of disciples with the aim of starting and building up churches that will reproduce. "Another change from the time of our parent's work to today," he said, "is that younger missionaries really want to work in teams. There are few leader types but many team player types, so all the missionaries in SEND Japan are assigned to a particular team for ministry, accountability, and care."

Japan still has a low percentage of believers, and there are some huge challenges now, he said. With a rapidly growing population, there are fewer and fewer Japanese pastors and leaders. How local churches will survive is a major issue.

* * * * *

Richard Nakamura served in Japan for twenty years as a missionary for SEND International. He is now doing Japanese Diaspora Ministries, working with Japanese living in the Seattle, Washington, area.

"I have total respect for those who came before me," he told me. "Other longtime missionaries have told me about the conditions in those early years. Missionaries like your folks dug the hard soil and made it tons easier to us missionaries that came afterward. I'm so grateful."

When comparing the work of early missionaries with today's missionaries, he said by the time he arrived in Japan in 1988, SEND had been focusing on planting churches for those who received Christ during the tent meeting era. Tracts and flyers may have been effective in the 1950s and 1960s, and many people came to know Christ through those tracts and flyers. But unfortunately, many other groups, including Christian, non-Christian, cults, businesses, "shady" businesses, etc., also used tracts to the point that people were tired of them, and people disposed of them quickly.

He recalled, "One of the churches received a large gift for evangelism. A special speaker was called and ten thousand tracts were ordered. Summer missionaries passed out tracts to all the *danchi*s, apartments, and houses along the train stations in the area.

"On that special day, we had one visitor, who only came once. What a shocking letdown. Of course, the event made us rethink what, why, and how we do things.

"There are still many missionaries and pastors who are stuck in the old paradigm, but the landscape has changed, so we need to think of ways that are relevant to the Japanese now. One of the things that I learned was that a transformed life speaks volumes. We need to better equip, enable, bless, and send out the believers to do the 'work' of evangelism and discipleship all around them.

"In the past, it was too pastor and missionary centric. Good intentions, but it kept the believers at an immature level. In order to mature as a disciple, we need to release them. They will make mistakes, but that is how we all learn. We did a good job of making church attendees but not mature disciples. There is a growing movement to change, but it's taking a lot of time.

"Focusing on being a transparent, true community is also important. In the past, people put on their happy faces and attended church. Many did not know of struggles, sickness, burdens, etc., because of the pressure to show a 'perfect' Christian.

"We are not perfect, and people know it. We need to be more authentic and be allowed to be 'weak,' which is why we need Christ. Churches are beginning to understand the importance of true community. When it's real, people around them will know.

"Many Japanese receive Christ outside of Japan. There is a wealth of resources there, but unfortunately, they are often discouraged and disillusioned with the Japanese church and leave (but not necessarily leave Christ). We need to welcome and bless them.

"When form is replaced by relationship (based on love and truth), things will change. I believe it is happening now but slowly.

"One key is not to have a 'come to church' mentality. The church needs to bring Jesus to the people. Have people minister in real and practical ways in their work places, schools, neighborhoods, and homes," he said.

Mom wrote, "There is a way, but people have to be willing to go. They have to be willing to learn a new language, be a part of a team, and start with absolutely nothing but God's grace and direction to see churches established. Young couples who are not intimidated in any way are needed to work in a country like Japan where Buddhism continues to grow more and more each day, where more and more young Japanese are returning to their traditionally strong, religiously binding ways.

"Who among you will go to these who have heard and not received the Word of the Lord Jesus, or who have never heard and are searching for the truth to get free from the lives they have been living?

"I am convinced that there are young people with a burden to reach the lost in Japan and would be willing to go if they knew they could reach so many for the Lord.

"Prayer in this is the key. Then the Lord will speak to hearts. The Word of the Lord is key to changing lives because Jesus Never Fails."

POSTSCRIPT

M ost of what Mom wrote here led up to and ended in 1986, but that didn't mean that God was finished with them. They still were living in Mesa, Arizona, when Arizona College of the Bible (ACB) in Phoenix asked Dad to come on board and develop a computer software package for the college to use in their student registration process. Dad had taught himself a bit of computer programming several years earlier, and he created a program that worked for ACB's registration needs. He also was coleader for a group of ACB students that went on a mission trip to Micronesia, including Palau, where he had been stationed briefly during the war.

At the same time, Mom was able to return to college, as she had not completed her degree from Columbia Bible College before they left for Japan in 1951. She earned her degree when she was sixty.

In 1988, Mom and Dad were invited to work at Tyndale Theological Seminary in the Netherlands by Dr. Art Johnson, founding president of the seminary.

A confession needs to be included here. I asked Linda and Tim if they knew what Mom and Dad did at Tyndale because I wasn't sure, and apparently, none of us were exactly sure. So after making contact with the seminary more than twenty years after the fact, they found several people that had worked alongside Mom and Dad. They were kind enough to share their thoughts.

* * * * *

Roger and Margaret were among the many retired missionaries who volunteered time and energy in those early days to help the seminary get established. They made significant contributions in that respect. Margaret was like a mother to many students, both men and women, who were far from home and family. I know that she maintained correspondence with many of them after they returned to the United States. Roger did a lot to keep the physical plant in order and supplied with necessary materials. He was a great encourager to all of us.

Keith and Nancy Chrisman.

* * * * *

There were many retirees who came to Tyndale to assist as their second or third career. We were young and nearly right out of school. Roger served as Tyndale's facility manager, and Meg was President Johnson's receptionist and alumni correspondent. Besides serving alongside Roger and Meg at Tyndale, they were our neighbors in the little town of Badhoevedorp just south of Amsterdam. They were like grandparents to our boys. Meg almost always attended a women's handcraft evening that met in our home. She adopted many of the young mothers from the neighborhood who came to the meeting. We did a lot of quilting, and before she left, the girls presented her with a red-and-blue log cabin quilt with hearts in the center of each block. Meg was a true prayer warrior and letter writer, a lost art. I'm sure there are many Tyndale alumni that she wrote to and prayed for faithfully. They touched so many lives and were a blessing shared around the world.

Creig and Sherry Marlowe.

* * * * *

In 1993, Mom and Dad were invited to be Distinguished Missionaries in Residence at Lancaster Bible College in Lancaster, Pennsylvania. They had known LBC president Dr. Gilbert A. Peterson from their time in Arizona. President Peterson recognized the value they could bring to the students at LBC with their wisdom and experiences. They started the International Student Fellowship and taught an evangelism and church-planting course. They also were advisors to international students and missionary kids.

Dad went to be with the Lord in October 1995 when he was seventy years old. Mom continued with the Student Services Department until she retired in 2006 at age eighty-two. Following that, Mom continued to stay in touch with many of her students around the world.

While part of this book had its genesis in that term paper, it wasn't until after she retired that she decided to write a book of their experiences as missionaries. And she decided to start the book of their missionary journey at the beginning of their lives as a way to help explain how they grew up and became the people that they did to pack up a young family, travel to a foreign country, and serve the Lord.

Nine years after Dad passed, God brought another man into Mom's life. Earl Shaiebly had been born and raised in the Lancaster area, and he had been alone for a number of years after Vera, his companion and wife of fifty-seven years, had passed.

Earl wrote in his memoirs,

> Since then (the death of his wife), there were lonely times for me, yet the Lord brought comfort and peace to my soul. I did a lot of talking with Him. So as long as God lets me on this earth, I want to walk in fellowship with Him and the best I know how, to be obedient to and serve Him. Without Him I would be very miserable. He has promised to meet my needs and I am thankful for His presence in my life.
>
> In November 2003, He did meet a need as I became acquainted with a lovely lady, Meg Fox, while sitting beside her in our Sunday school class. In the following months, a friendship grew into a love relationship. We just thank God for

bringing us together. It is a blessing from the Lord at this time of our lives. We are so very happy together.

On June 4, 2004, we became married at Calvary Church in Lancaster. We are thankful for the support of all our family members and also from our friends.

They were eighty-one and eighty years old when they married and for the next eleven years brought much joy into each other's lives. When Mom was eighty-five, she told me in confidence that she may not finish this book before she died. I encouraged her to write as much as she could, and if she didn't complete it, I would finish it for her.

Mom went to be with the Lord in August 2015 at age ninety-one. Earl followed in January 2017.

Linda joined Mom and Dad in May 2019.

EDITOR'S ACKNOWLEDGMENTS

*J*esus Never Fails was a work of love that took decades to write, beginning when Mom and Dad decided to dedicate their lives to the Lord's work and the time they allowed God to do many works in their lives. Mom and Dad touched many lives during their lifetime, and there would never be enough paper to mention all of those people that had a hand in molding their lives from the time they were children until the time they went to be with the Lord.

However, there are some people I would like to thank for their invaluable assistance in editing this book. Finding people to verify and clarify what Mom had written sometimes was a challenge as many of her peers too have passed.

I believe that Mom not only wanted this book to be a historical account of how the Lord worked in their lives on and off the field but also an invitation and encouragement to others to go into full-time Christian work, whether as missionaries wherever God sends them, or as pastors of churches, prayer warriors, and financial supporters of those doing God's work.

If you feel called to be a missionary, *go*. You will be able to accomplish all that the Lord sets in front of you. If you want to be a prayer partner for the mission field, *pray*. Prayer lets the Lord know that you are on the missionary's team. And whatever God puts on your heart, *give*. Your financial gifts make missionary work possible.

With that in mind, I would like to thank Jon Reasoner and Richard Nakamura for their insights and input into working on the mission field today.

Ken Reddington, another boyhood friend in Japan, is the missionary pastor at Tenno New Life Chapel in Kochi, Japan. Thank you, Ken, for translating the songs that were included in this book.

Thanks to Dick Mills with SEND International, who provided time lines of Mom and Dad's time with FEGC/SEND.

Thank you goes to Keith and Nancy Chrisman and Creig and Sherry Marlowe from Tyndale Theological Seminary for sharing their thoughts on Mom and Dad's time in Holland.

And thank you for reading this book.

ABOUT THE AUTHOR

M argaret Fox Shaiebly had dreams and aspirations of being a missionary to Borneo. She thought nursing school would help her treat people, and she figured she would have to become a pilot to reach distant tribal members. She had attended church regularly since she was a child, but it wasn't until an encounter at a Bible camp as a teenager that she knew she wasn't a true believer in Jesus Christ.

Margaret and her husband Roger dedicated their lives to serving as missionaries for forty-four years in Japan, the United States, and in Holland. She retired as missionary in residence at Lancaster Bible College in Pennsylvania at age eighty-two and went to be with the Lord at ninety-one.

CPSIA information can be obtained
at www.ICGtesting.com
Printed in the USA
FSHW012129060521
81116FS